THE SMART TRADER'S PLAYBOOK

Proven Strategies to Win in Any Market

BlueRose ONE.com
Stories Matter
NewDelhi • London

BLUEROSE PUBLISHERS
India | U.K.

BlueRose ONE.com
Stories Matter
NewDelhi • London

For permissions requests or inquiries regarding this publication, please contact:

BLUEROSE PUBLISHERS
www.BlueRoseONE.com
info@bluerosepublishers.com
+91 8882 898 898
+4407342408967

ISBN: 978-93-7310-498-0

First Edition: October 2025

Wise Investing

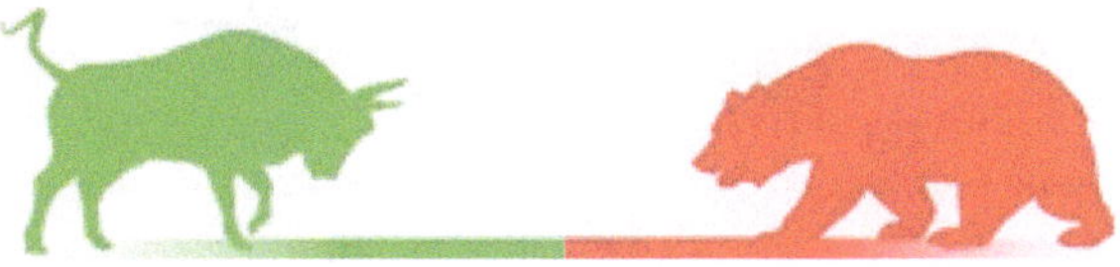

THE CANDLESTICK & CHART PATTERNS

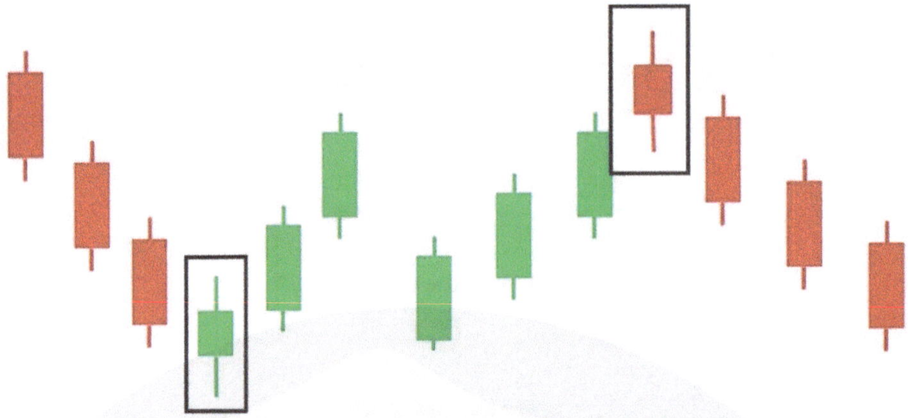

THE CANDLESTICK TRADING BIBLE

INVENTED BY MUNEHISA HOMMA

The most successful trader in history

Index

No. Content	Page no.
1. What is candlestick?	6
2. Type's of candlestick Pattern	
2.1 Hammer	8
2.2 Inverted hammer	9
2.3 Gravestone doji	10
2.4 Dragonfly feeding	11
2.5 Spinning top	12
2.6 Morning star	13
2.7 Evening star	14
2.8 Shooting star	15
2.9 Hanging man	16
2.10 Bullish engulfing	17
2.11 Bearish engulfing	18
2.12 Tweezer bottom	19
2.13 Tweezer top	20
2.14 Bullish inside bar	21
2.15 Bearish inside bar	22

2.16 Bullish Harami	23
2.17 Bearish Harami	24
2.18 Three white soldiers	25
2.19 Three black crows	26
2.20 Dark cloud cover	27
2.21 Pin bar	28
2.22 Bullish piercing	29
2.23 Bullish kicker	30
2.24 Bearish kicker.	31
2.25 Three outside up	32
2.26 Bearish Marubozu	33
2.27 Bullish Marubozu	34
3. Types of Chart Pattern	
3.1 Double Top Pattern	35
3.2 Double Bottom Pattern	36
3.3 Triple Top Pattern	37
3.4 Triple Bottom Pattern	38
3.5 Bullish Pennant	39
3.6 Bearish Pennant	40
3.7 Bullish Flag Pattern	41

3.8 Bearish Flag Pattern	42
3.9 Bullish Rectangle	43
3.10 Bearish Rectangle	44
3.11 Rising Wedge	45
3.12 Falling Wedge	46
3.13 Head and Shoulders	47
3.14 Inverted Head and Shoulders	48
3.15 Symmetrical Triangle	49
3.16 Ascending Triangle	50
3.17 Descending Triangle	51
3.18 Cup and Handle	52
3.19 Rounding Bottom	53
3.20 Diamond Top	54
3.21 Diamond Bottom	55

1. What is a Candlestick?

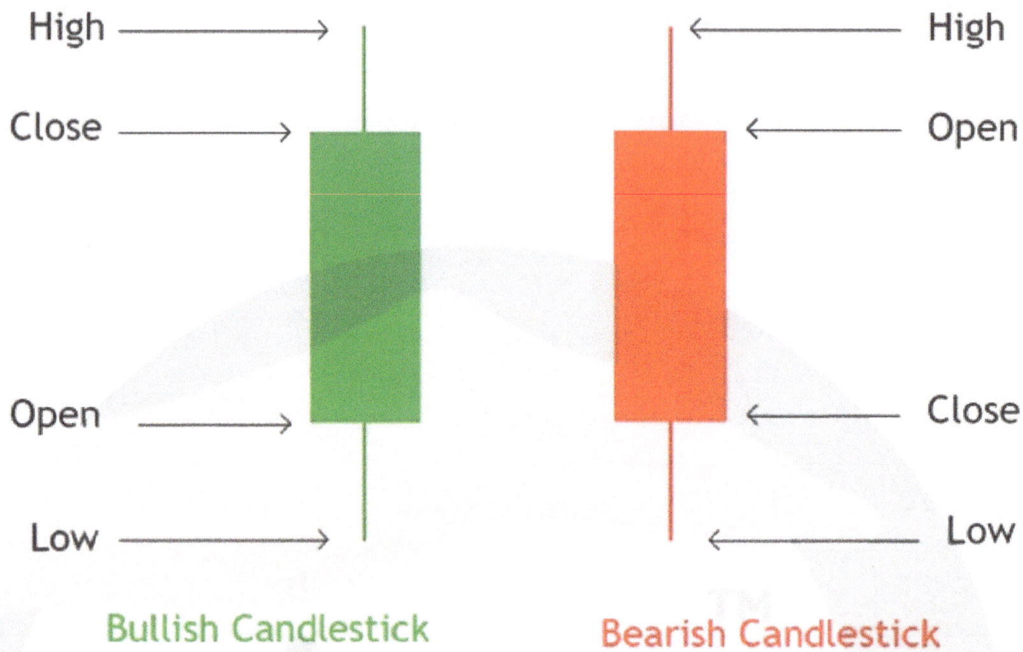

Candlesticks are used to understand trading patterns.
A **pattern** means a particular type of event that gives a specific signal. When such a signal appears, it is called a **pattern**. Technical analysts make their trading decisions based on these patterns.

A pattern can be formed by **two or more candlesticks**, but sometimes even a **single candlestick** can represent a pattern. That's why candlestick patterns are divided into:

- **Single candlestick patterns** – formed by one candlestick
- **Multiple candlestick patterns** – formed by two or more candlesticks.

A candlestick pattern shows the **high, low, open, and close price** of a day. All of this is captured in one candle.

- When the market opens, the first recorded price is the **open price**.
- As the price reaches its **highest point**, that is recorded as the **high price**.
- As the price drops to the **lowest point**, that becomes the **low price**.
- Finally, when the market closes, that is the **closing price**.

Thus, a single candlestick gives complete information about a day's trading.
But the stock market doesn't behave the same every day, so different candlestick patterns keep forming regularly.

If you understand the basics, there are mainly **two types of candlesticks**:

1. **Bullish Candle** – shown in **green**.
   - It represents all four price levels (open, high, low, close).
   - It means the candle closed **higher** than the previous candle's closing price.
2. **Bearish Candle** – shown in **red**.
   - It also shows the four price levels.
   - It means the candle closed **lower** than the previous candle's closing price.

2. Type's of candlestick pattern

2.1 Hammer

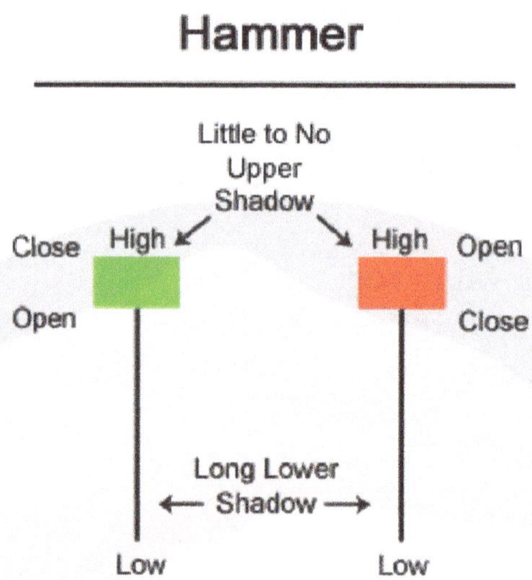

In a hammer candle, the body of the candle is small and the lower shadow is very long and there is no upper shadow at all, we call it a hammer candle. This type of candle can be of any colour either red or green. If a hammer candle is formed in a down trend in the chart, then there are 90% chances of the market going into an up trend in which the share price increases. If a hammer candle is formed in an up trend in the chart, then there are 90% chances of the market going into a down trend. This hammer works in both intraday and short term.

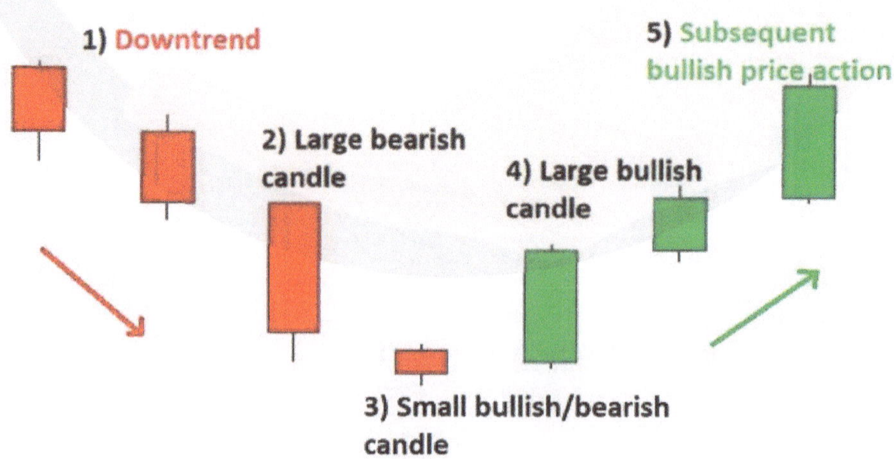

2.2 Inverted hammer

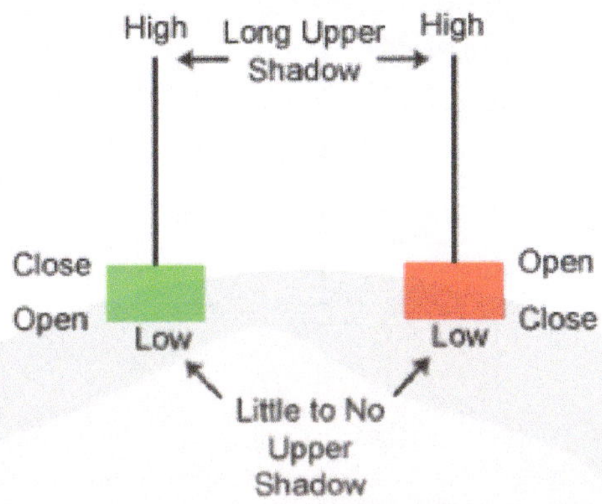

Inverted hammer is a bullish reversal pattern which indicates a rapid change in the market, the time of recession is over. The body of this candle is very small and the upper shadow is very large and the lower shadow is either absent or very small. It can be of any color. If this candlestick pattern is formed in the middle then it does not have much importance. The color of inverted hammer can be red or green. But the color of inverted hammer does not matter whether it is green or red but if the color of inverted hammer is green then it is better.

2.3 Gravestone doji

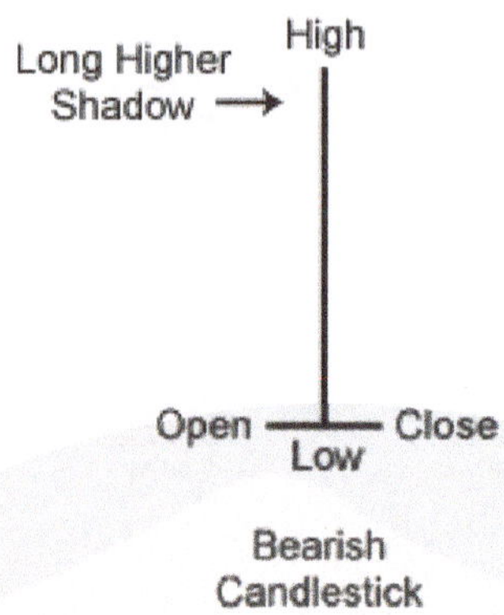

Gravestone Doji Market Sentiment Interpretation It is considered bearish and appears during an uptrade. The Gravestone Doji is formed when the open, low, and close are the same. Often, the candlestick has no real body and a long upper shadow, making it look like an inverted 'T'.

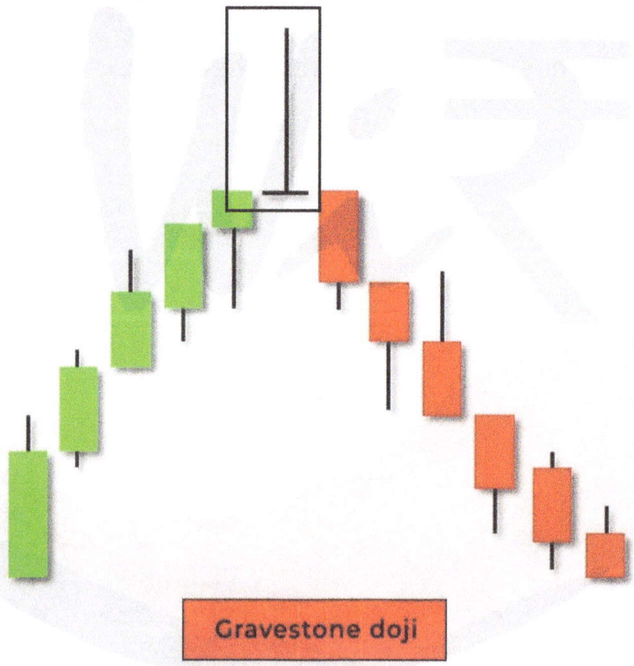

This gravestone doji is just a symbol of bearish trend. This candle means that when the bullish trend in the market is about to end, then gravestone doji is formed and the market becomes more bullish. You can easily identify it because there is no lower shadow in it, only its high and close are visible.

2.4 Dragonfly feeding

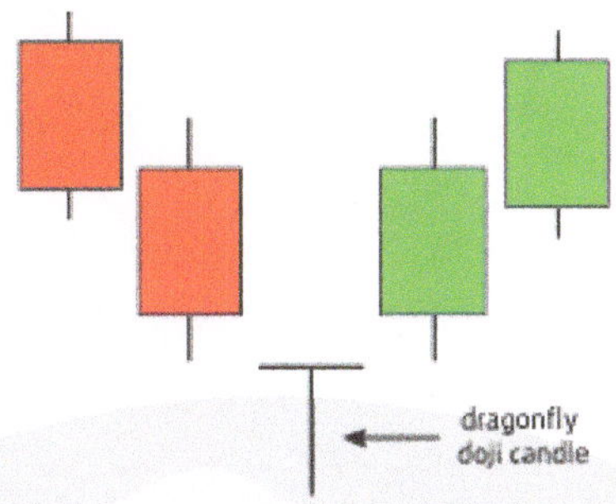

The pattern of the Dragonfly Doji is like a candle with no real structure. It is a long downward reflection. A long downward bar appears during the Dragonfly uptrend, giving investors a hint that the bearish trend may gain strength and the uptrend may reverse. Investors always wait for the next candle to form after the Doji to confirm the trend.

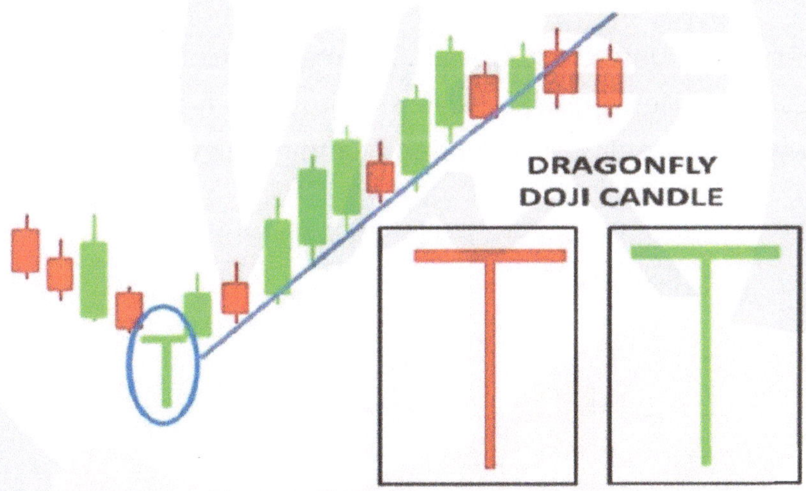

2.5 Spinning top

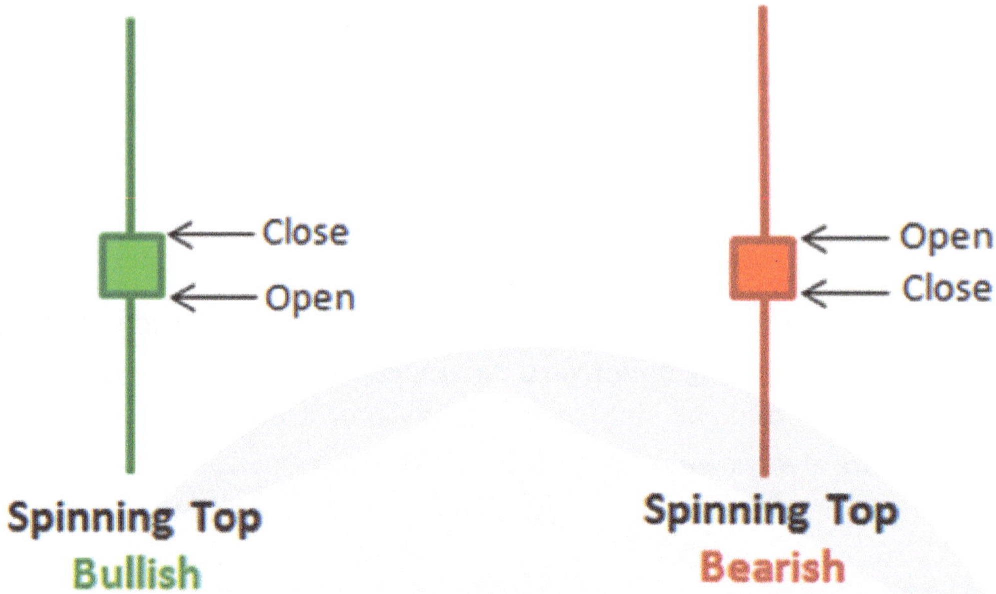

Its unique appearance is due to pressure in the market from both buyers and sellers. Buyers try to push the price up, while sellers try to push it down, but both fail to sustain the change. The result is a small body candlestick with long shadows on either side.

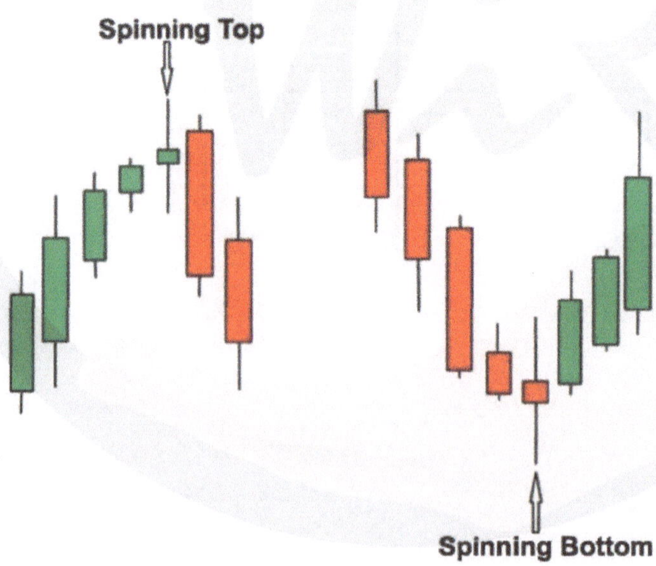

2.6 Morning star

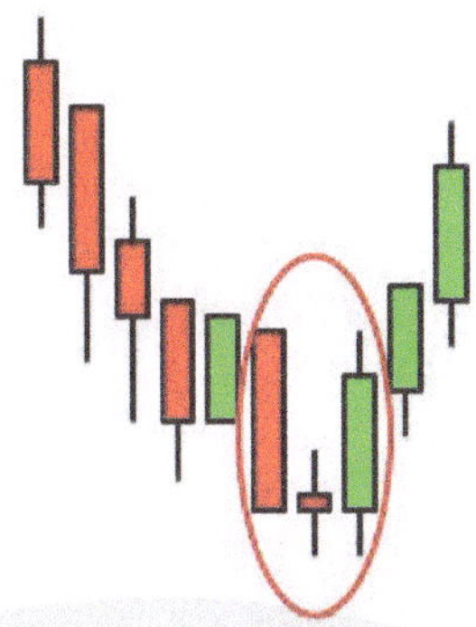

A normal candle is formed by one or two candles, but the morning star candle pattern is formed by three candles. The meaning of the morning star candle is "morning star" which is also called the Sun. In the morning star candle, the first candle can be long bearish, the second candle can be bullish or bearish and the third candle is long bullish. The morning star candle pattern is a bullish candle. When a good morning star candle is formed in the chart, then the possibility of a rise in the stock increases.

You can make good profits by doing intraday and swing trading with the Morning Star candle. If you are looking at this candle in intraday, then you should look at the 10 minute chart and if you are looking for swing trading, then you should look at the 1 day chart.

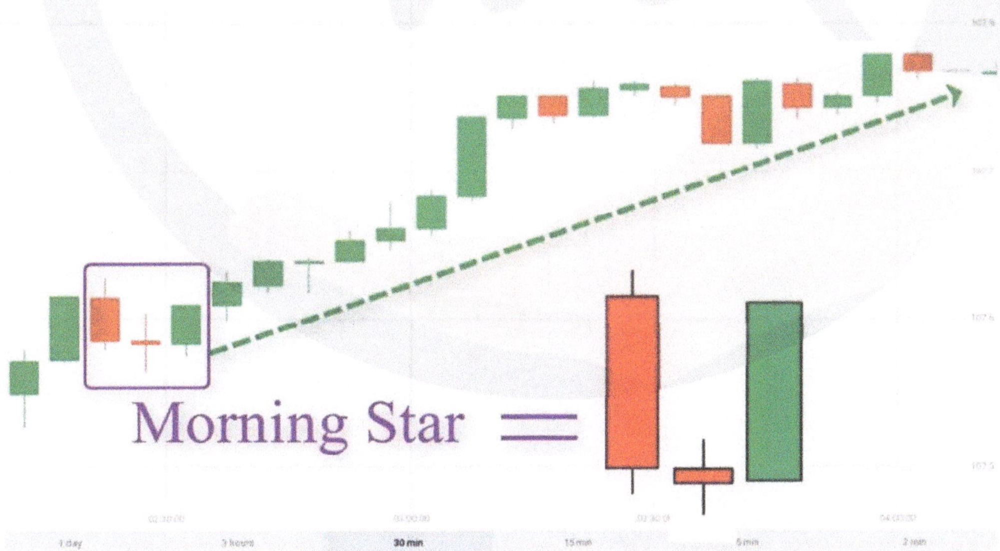

2.7 Evening star

The Evening star is a Bearish and Multiple Candlestick Pattern, which is formed by three consecutive candles in a chart, along with this, Evening star is also called UP TREND Reversal Pattern, it means that after seeing The Evening star Candlestick Pattern, BEARISH (Bearish) pattern can be seen in the stock in future,

The market is in UP trend and the bulls have complete control. The first candle of the Evening Star is a bullish candle which shows the strength of the bullish market and also gives the message that more and more people want to buy the stock. The third candle of the Evening Star is a bearish candle with a gap up opening which shows the return of the bears in the market.

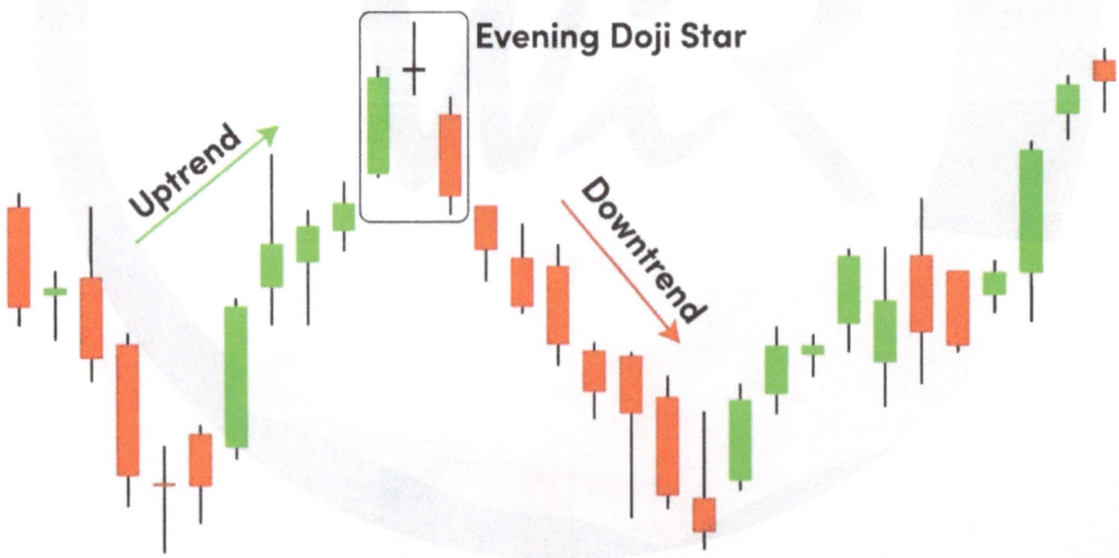

2.8 shooting star

Shooting star candle is formed at the top. It is formed at the top after a big rally in the market. Its volume is more than the previous candle. To take a trade here, the open price of the second new candle should be at the close price of the shooting star. When the new candle goes below the low price of the shooting star candle, a selling position should be created and a stop-loss should be placed at the high price of the shooting star. Shooting star candle pattern is formed on intraday charts, daily charts and weekly charts. If you do intraday trading, then it should be seen on 5 minute, 10 minute or 15 minute charts and if you do positional trading, then it should be seen on daily or weekly charts.

2.9 Hanging man

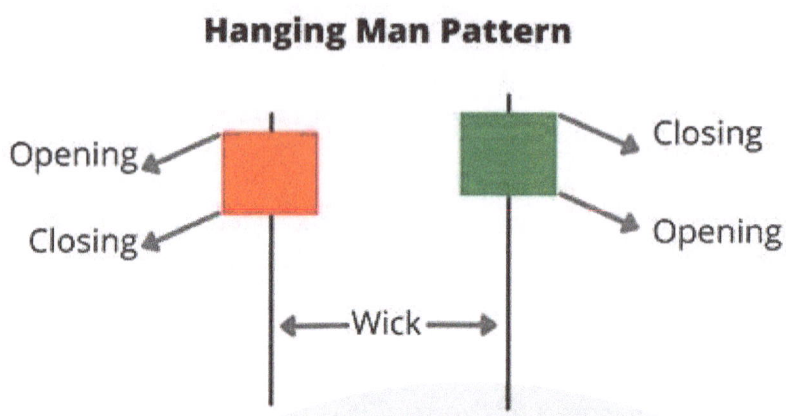

Hanging Man is a bearish pattern which is mostly formed in a strong uptrend and indicates a fall in the market as the selling pressure starts increasing. A hanging man candle is formed as soon as the uptrend ends.

This is a very bearish pattern, the shadow below it is very long, sellers pull the share price down and buyers try to take the price up but they cannot take it up, so never buy shares in a hanging bearish pattern. In the hanging man candle, you will not see the shadow at all or it will be very small. You have to keep one thing in mind that the color does not mean anything in this, it can be of both red and green color.

2.10 Bullish engulfing

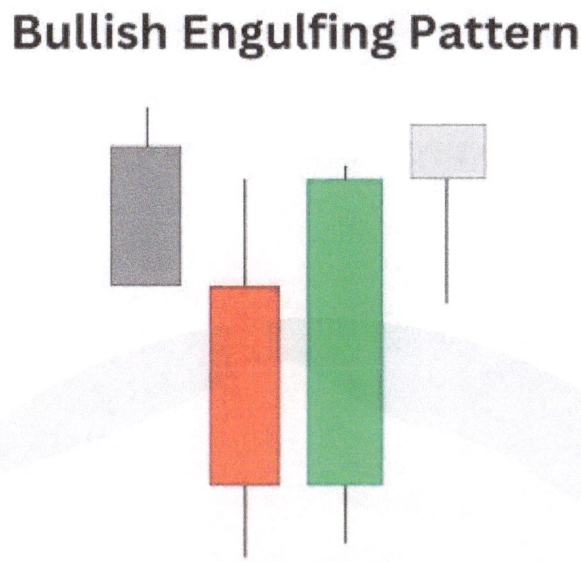

A bullish engulfing pattern is a two-candle reversal signal in technical analysis where a small bearish (red) candle is followed by a larger bullish (green) candle that completely covers the body of the prior candle. This pattern signals a shift in market sentiment from selling to buying, indicating a strong potential for the price to reverse from a downtrend to an uptrend.

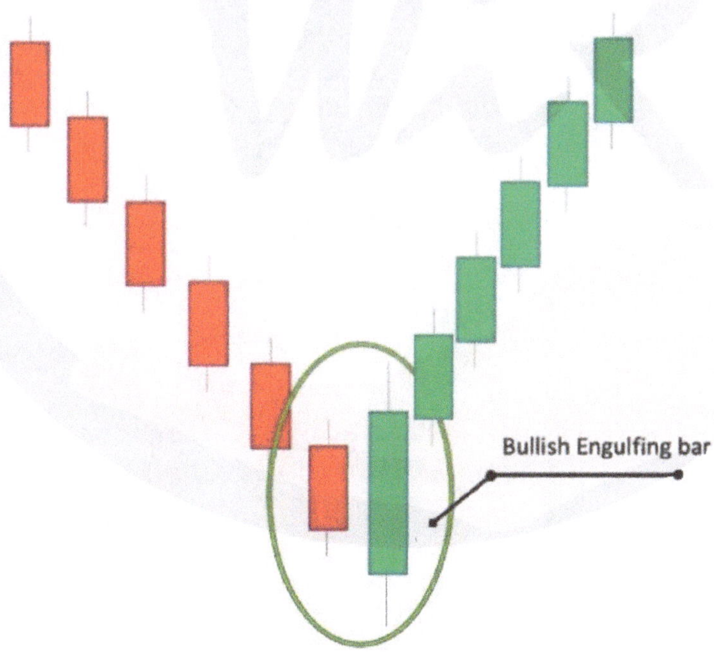

2.11 Bearish engulfing

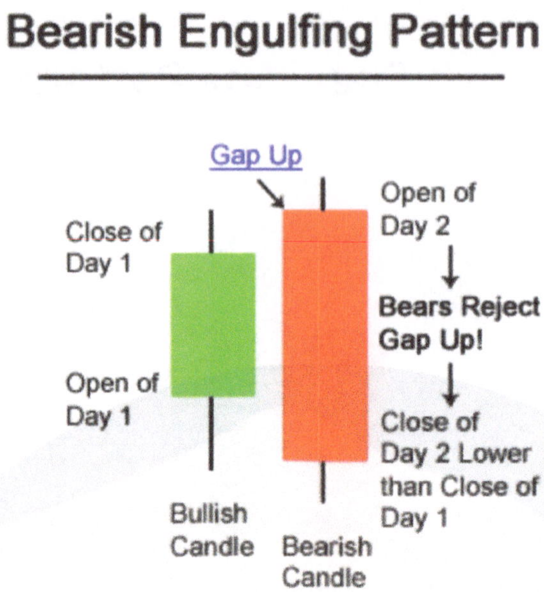

A bearish engulfing pattern is a technical analysis candlestick chart pattern that signals a potential reversal from an uptrend to a downtrend. It occurs after a bullish (up) candle is followed by a larger bearish (down) candle that completely engulfs the first candle's body, indicating that selling pressure has overcome buying pressure and the market sentiment is shifting downwards.

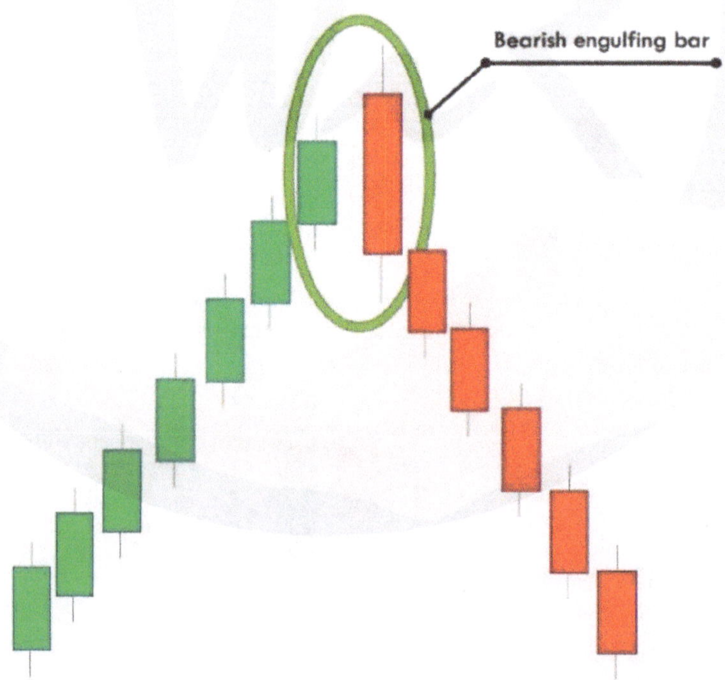

2.12 Tweezer bottom

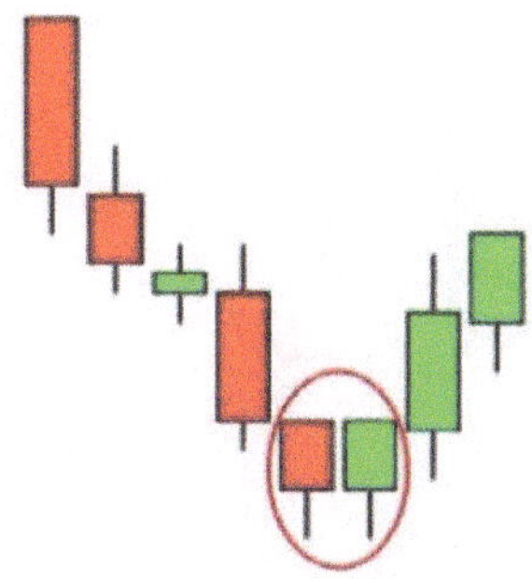

Tweezer Bottoms

Two-way bottom is a bullish pattern. This pattern is formed when sellers are pushing the price downwards even after a long bearish trend in the stock market but sellers are not able to keep the price down at the end of the session. This means that the bearish trend is over now and the bullish trend is about to begin.

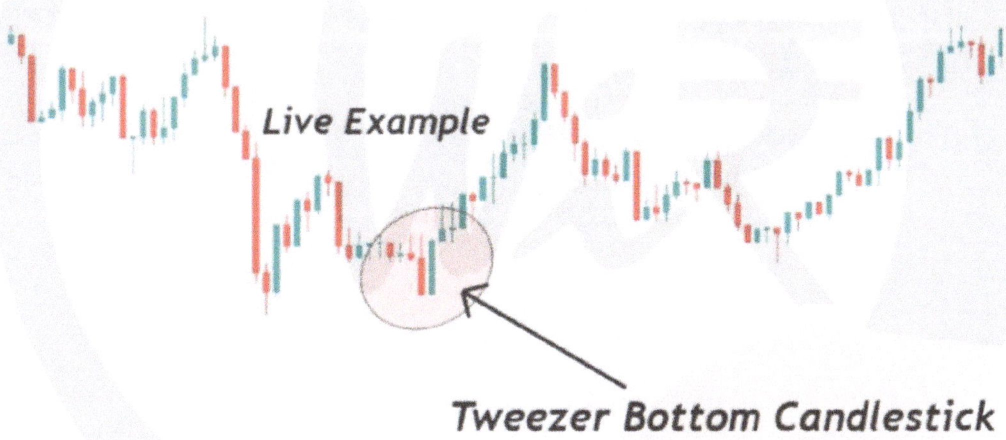

2.13 Tweezer top

Tweezer Top Candlestick Pattern is a double candlestick pattern. Its first candle is a bullish green candle and the second is bearish i.e. red. It is always formed on the 'top' of the chart after a long uptrend. The first candle of this pattern can be a long bullish, small bullish or any single bullish candle. The second candle after this can also be a long bearish, small bearish or any single bearish candle.

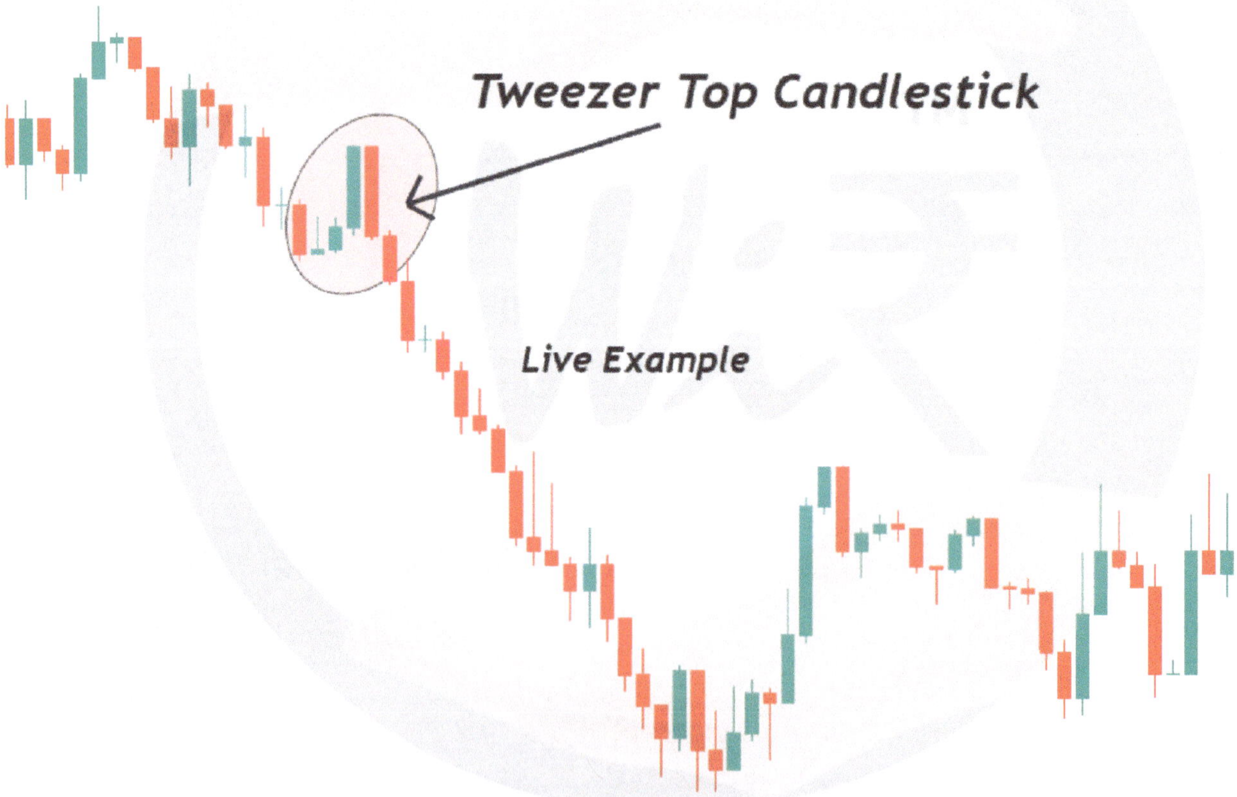

2.14 Bullish inside bar

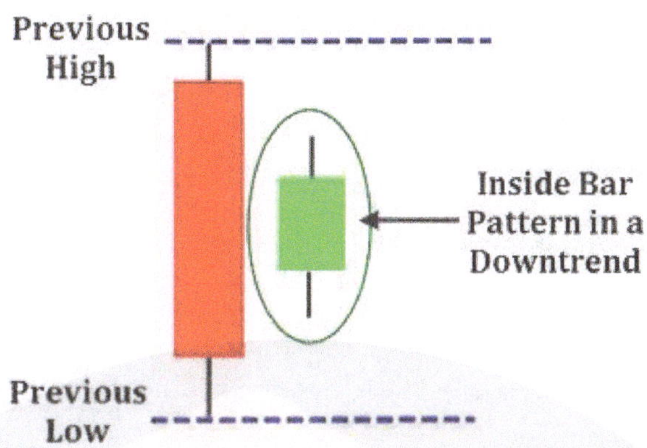

An inside bar chart pattern is contained within a larger candle, some call it the mother bar. It is a pattern that forms after a large move in the market and represents a period of consolidation, with the next candle being a BULLISH one.

2.15 Bearish inside bar

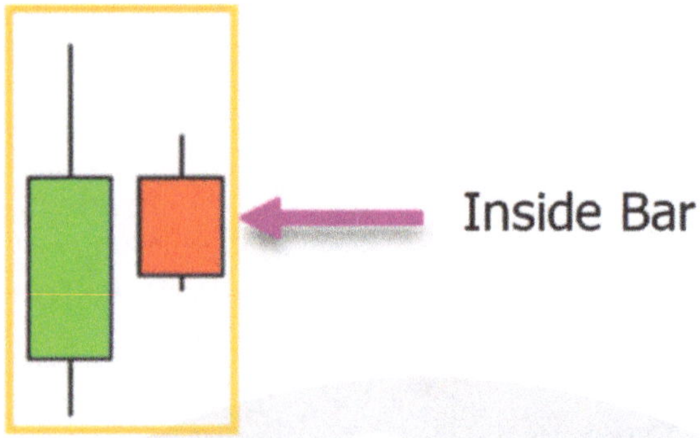

An inside bar chart pattern is a pattern that forms within a larger candle. Some call it a mother bar. It is a pattern that forms after a large move in the market and represents a period of consolidation, with the next candle being BEARISH. Incorporating inside bar strategy within a trading system can enhance a trader's market analysis technique.

2.16 Bullish Harami

The first candle is a large candle and the second candle is much smaller than the first candle and the colour of both the candles is different. HARAMI PATTERN is formed in both types of TREND i.e. UP TREND and DOWN TREND. If HARAMI PATTERN is formed in DOWNTREND in the chart then there is a possibility of TREND REVERSAL i.e. BULLISH TREND in future. Bullish harami candle is a bullish candlestick pattern, i.e. it shows bullishness. When this candle is formed then it shows that the bearish period in the stock is over and the bullishness has started.

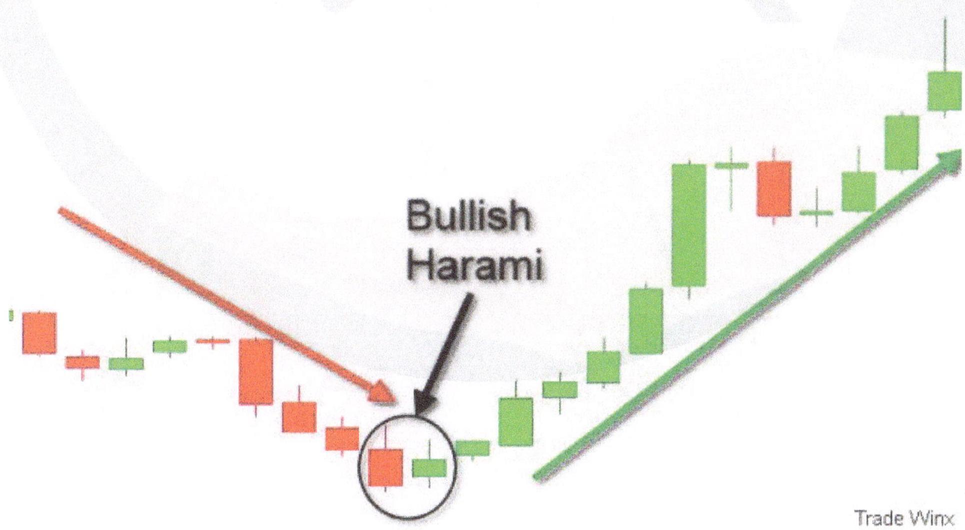

2.17 Bearish Harami

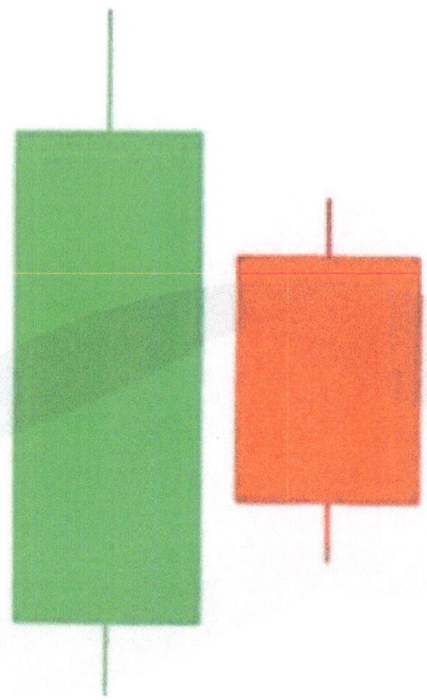

The first candle is a large candle, and the second candle is much smaller than the first candle, and the colour of both the candles is different, HARAMI PATTERN is formed in both types of TREND i.e. UP TREND and DOWN TREND, and if HARAMI PATTERN is formed in UP TREND in the chart, then there is a possibility of TREND REVERSAL i.e. BERARISH TREND in future.

2.18 Three white soldiers

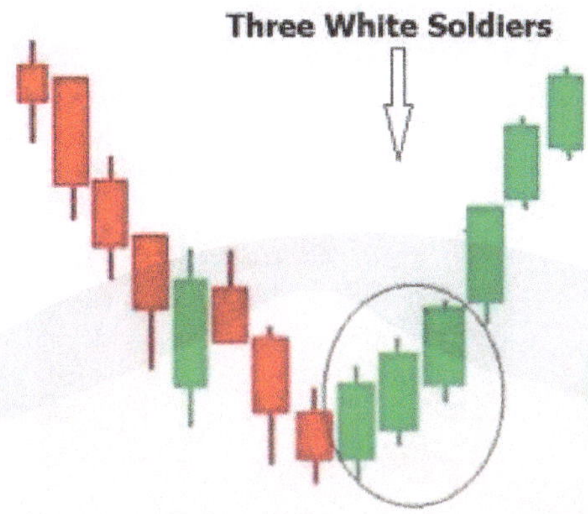

Mr White Soldiers is a 3 candle cluster pattern that signals price growth. They appear in a downtrend and warn of a possible reversal to an uptrend. This pattern indicates a bearish to bullish trade reversal signal.

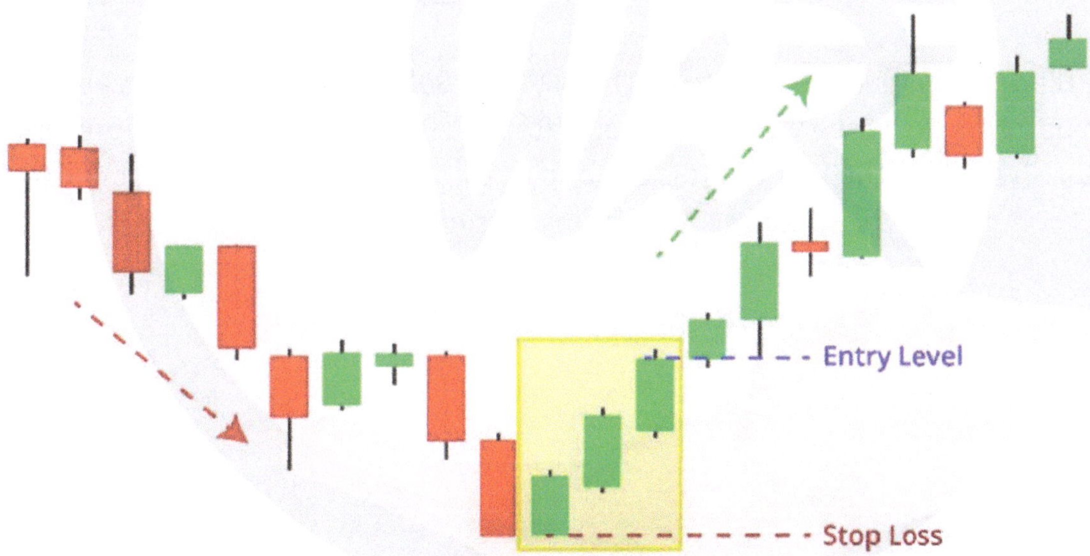

Fig. Three White Soldiers

2.19 Three black crows

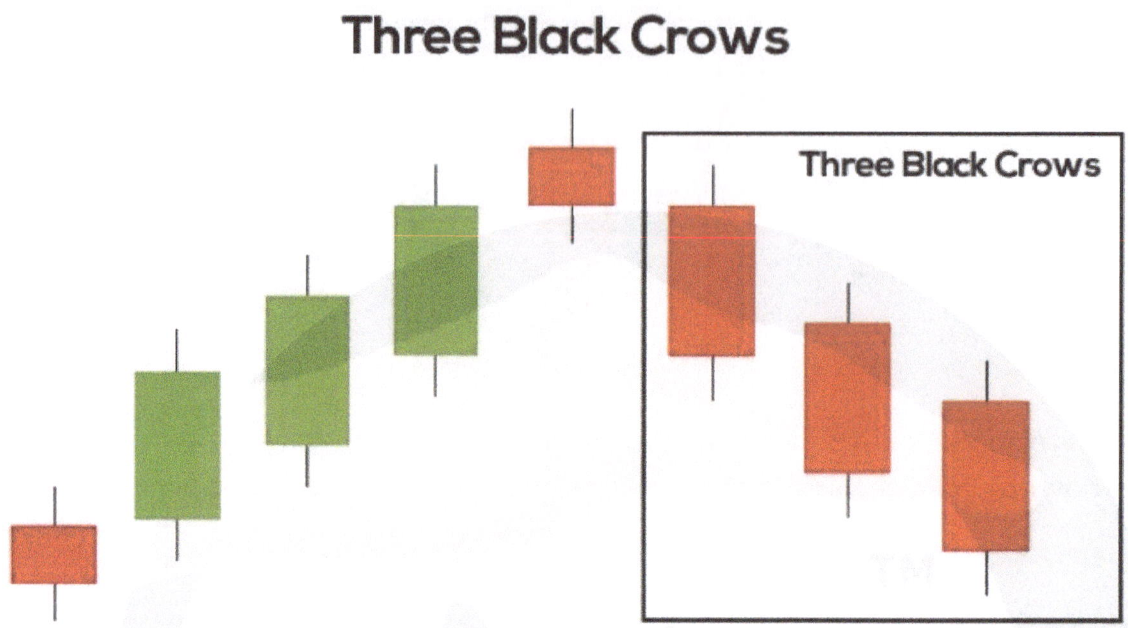

Three Black Crows is the opposite of Three White Soldiers which appears at the end of an uptrend. So, when we say the opposite. Mr. Black Crow Pattern represents a bearish trend in the market. It is a group of three long body candlesticks with consecutive falling closing prices.

2.20 Dark cloud cover

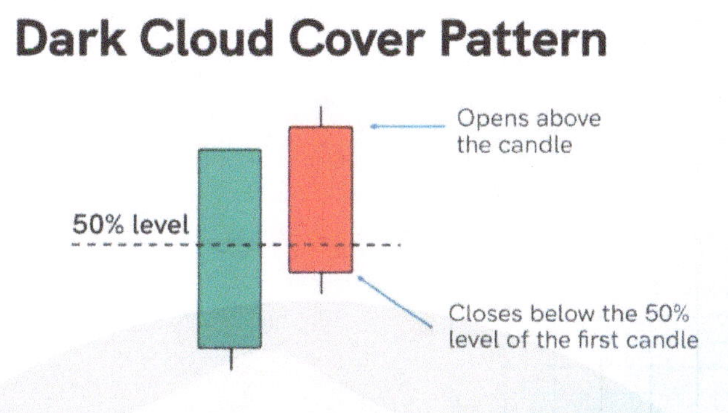

Dark Cloud Cover is a bearish reversal candlestick pattern that forms at the end of an uptrend. It is composed of two candlesticks. The first candlestick is a bookish candlestick and the second is a bearish candlestick. Traders find this pattern important as it signals a reversal of an uptrend into a downtrend.

2.21 Pin bar

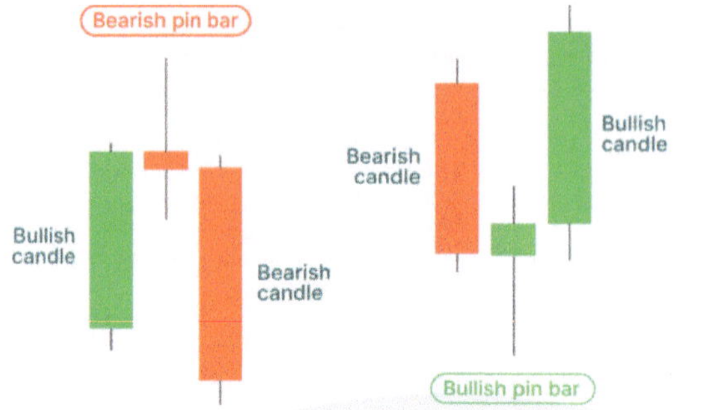

On this candlestick, there is a small part called the "nose". The nose is smaller than the other two parts. A Pin Bar is seen with its tail pointing down and the body pointing up. This means that the price is falling down but one side tries to pull it back.

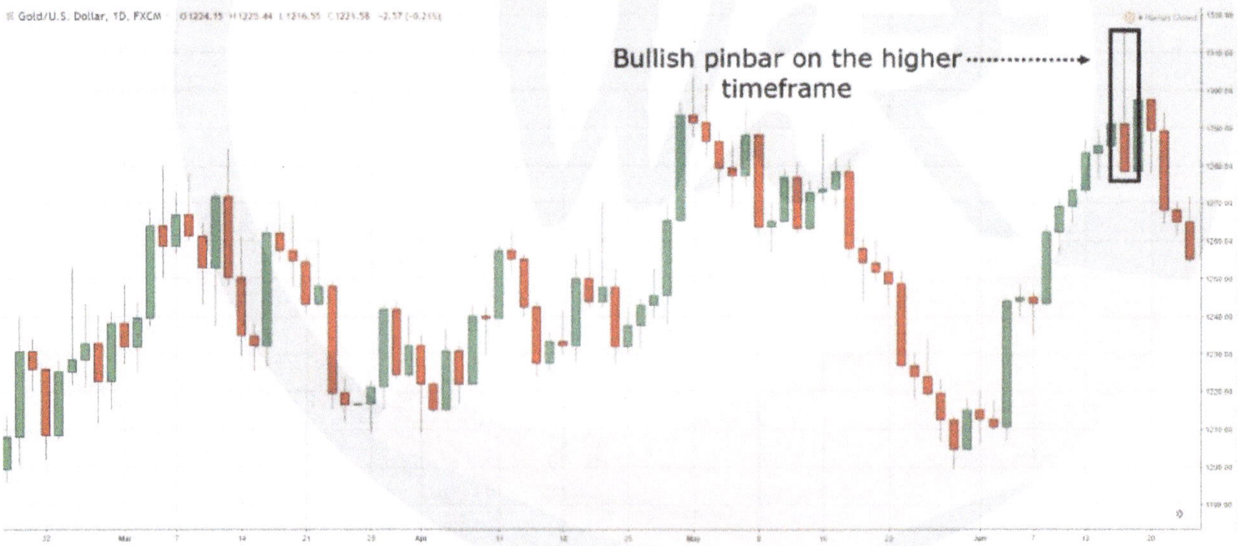

2.22 Bullish piercing

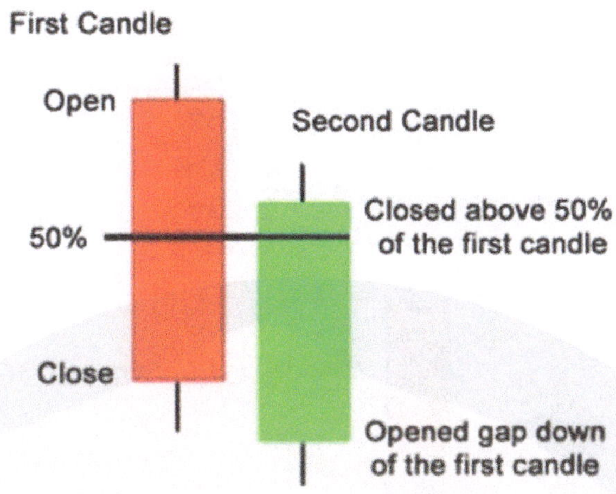

The piercing pattern is a bullish reversal pattern that can be found at the end of a downtrend. This candlestick pattern is used as an indicator to enter a long position or exit a sell position. The piercing pattern is formed when both bulls and bears are fighting for control of the prices. The piercing pattern is made up of two candlesticks, the first is bearish and the second is bullish candlestick.

2.23 Bullish kicker

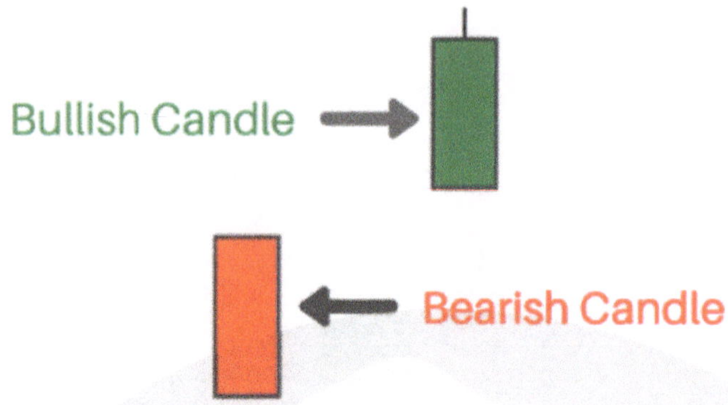

This pattern is characterized by a sharp reversal in price over the period of two candlesticks. Traders use the kicker pattern to determine which group of market participants is in control of the direction.

2.24 Bearish kicker

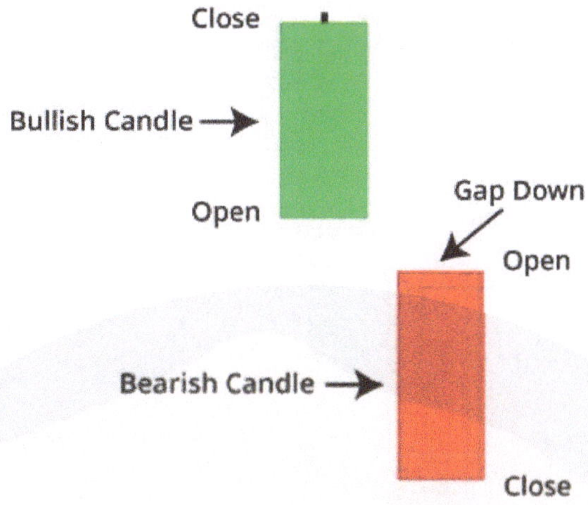

This pattern is characterized by a sharp reversal in price over a period of two candlesticks. Traders use the kicker pattern to determine which group of market participants is in control of the direction.

2.25 Three outside up

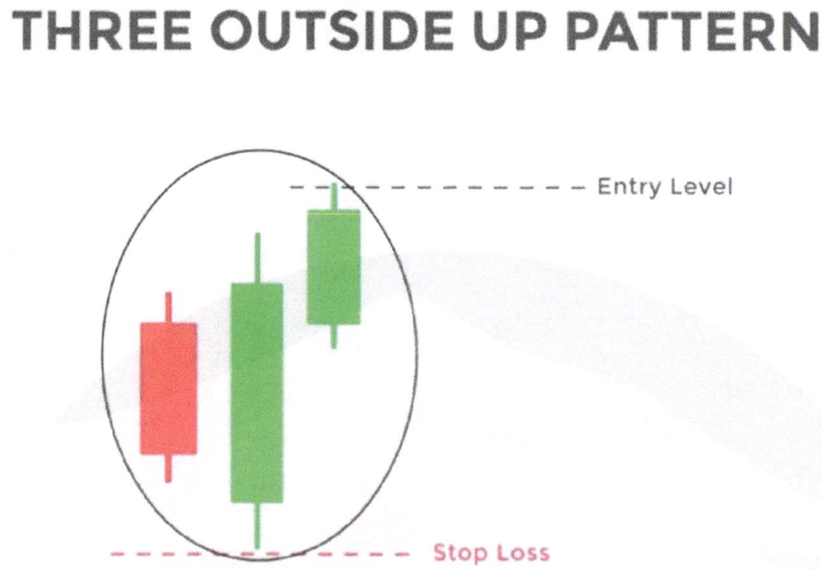

A key feature of this technical indicator is that its strength is determined by the size of the engulfing candlestick, which is the second of three. The larger the second candle the more significant it is outside of the three pattern.

2.26 Bearish Marubozu

The open price of a Bearish Marubozu Candle is above and the close is below and a perfect Bearish Marubozu candle does not have any upper or lower shadow. This means that the high is where it opens and the low is where it closes. But practically, even if there are some upper and lower shadows, it is called a Marubozu candlestick.

2.27 Bullish Marubozu

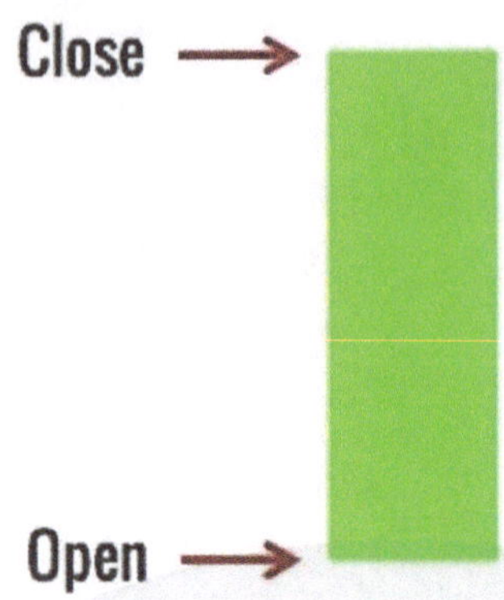

In a bullish marubozu candle, the open price and low price remain the same but the close price and high price are not the same. This candle has a shadow slightly above it, which should be 2 to 3% of the shadow body. When this candle opens in the chart, the buyers have a strong hold but at the time of closing, the sellers dominate a little.

3.Types of Chart Pattern

3.1 Double top Pattern

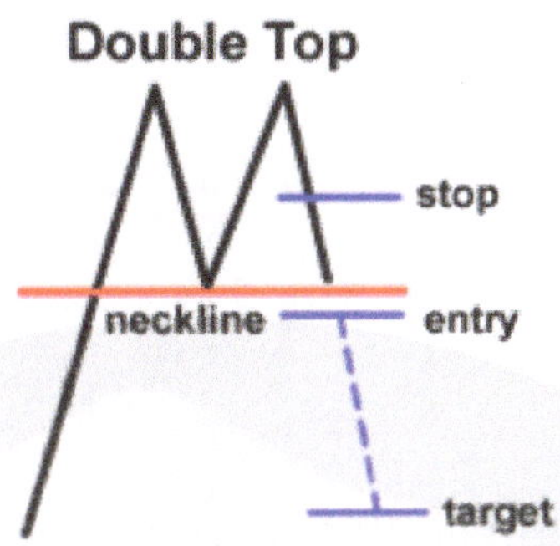

This pattern appears like the shape of the letter 'M' on a candlestick chart. According to this pattern, when a stock, after remaining at a certain price for a long time, goes up to a certain price and then comes down to a price and stops for some time and then goes up to the same place from where it had come down, and after stopping there for some time, comes down again to the same place from where it had gone up earlier, then this pattern is considered complete.

3.2 Double Bottom Pattern

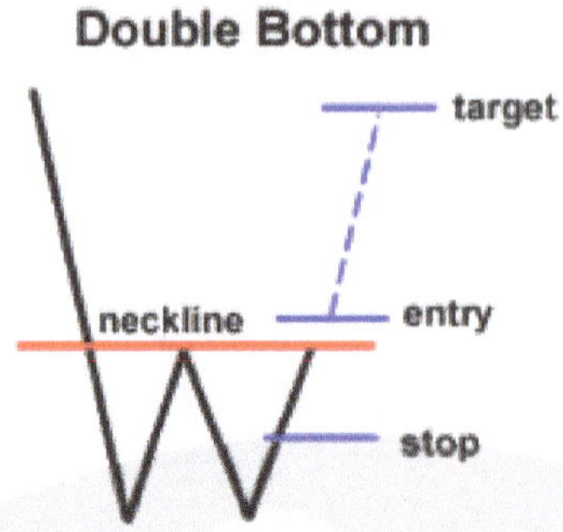

The English letter 'W', Double Bottom Pattern indicates that the share price will now go up. If the share price is falling and while falling it stops at a point, i.e. it forms a bottom, then starts moving upwards from there and while moving it stops at a point, then it goes down from there, waits for some time and then moves upwards and reaches the same price from where it had fallen, then in such a situation it is highly expected that now this share will only move upwards, meaning that now its price is going to increase a lot.

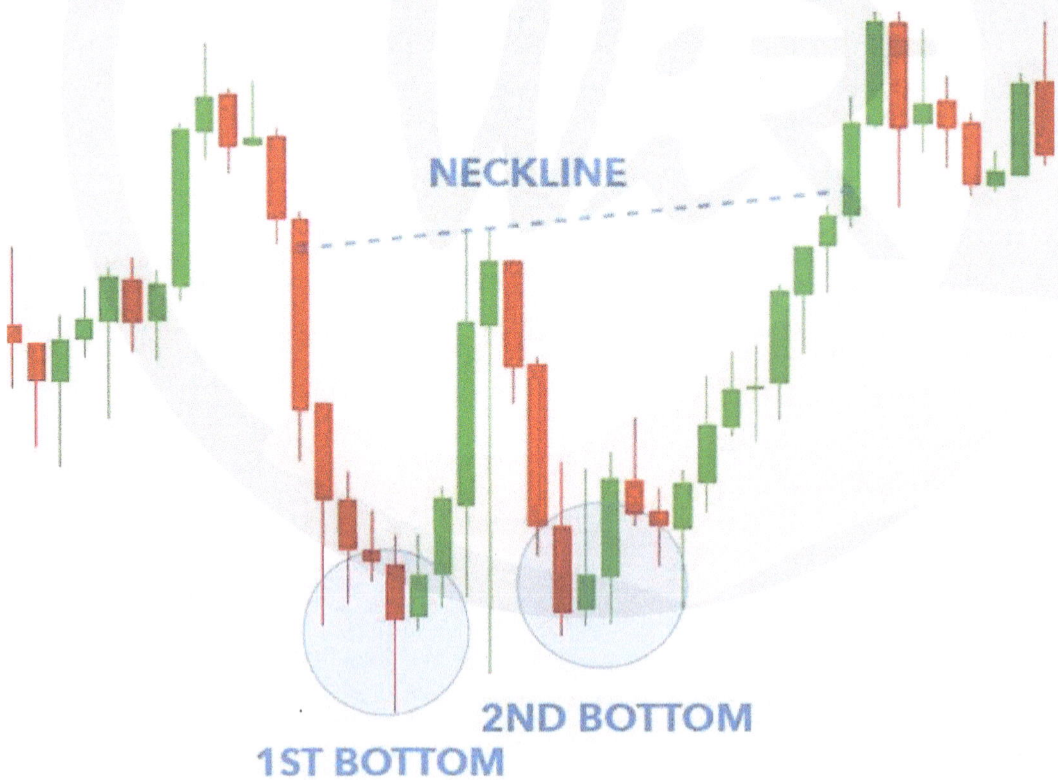

3.3 Triple Top

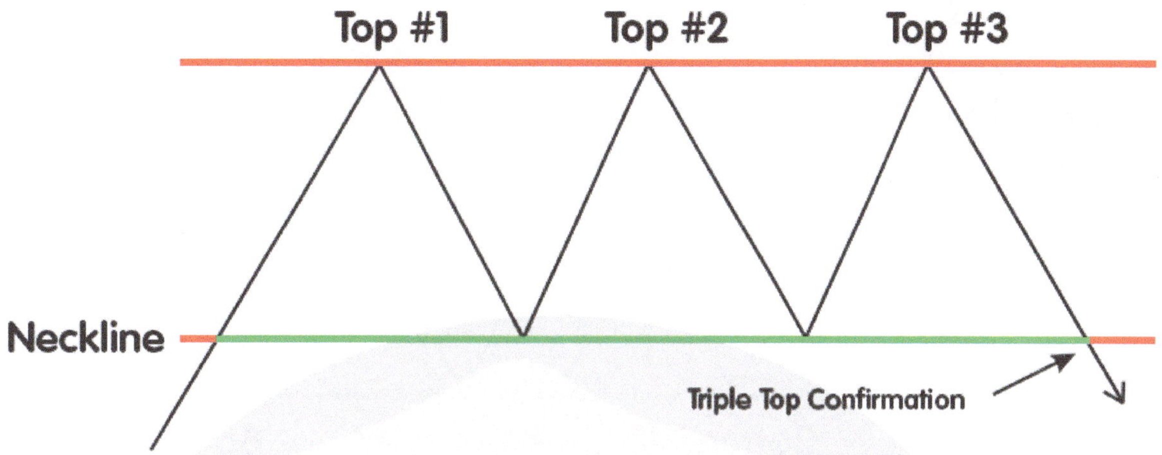

The triple top chart pattern is a reliable indicator that signals a trader to sell. It essentially tells a trader that after attempts to push prices up, there are signs that the asset is not worth much, and is unable to find buyers at that specific price level.

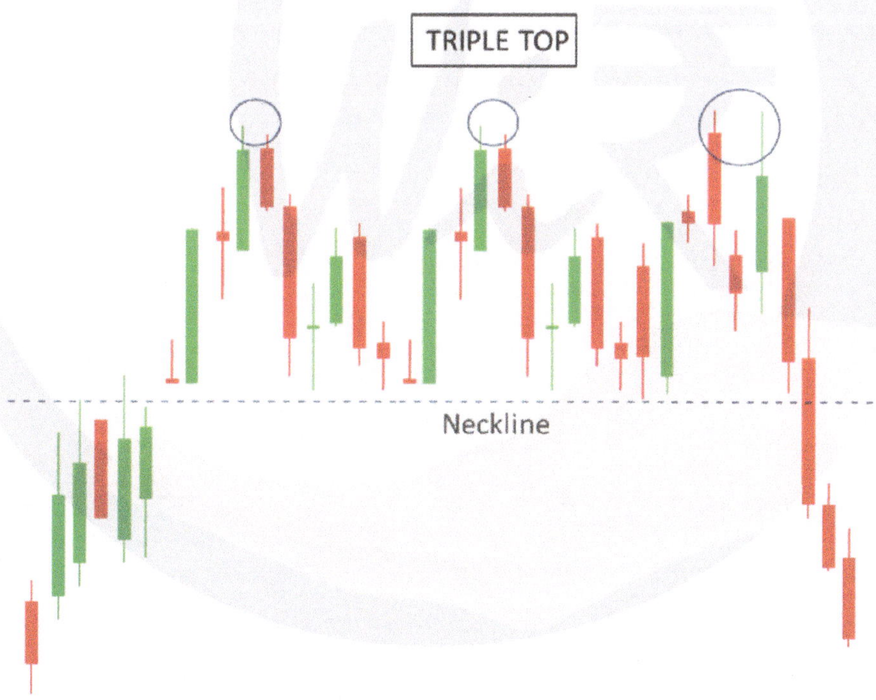

3.4 Triple Bottom

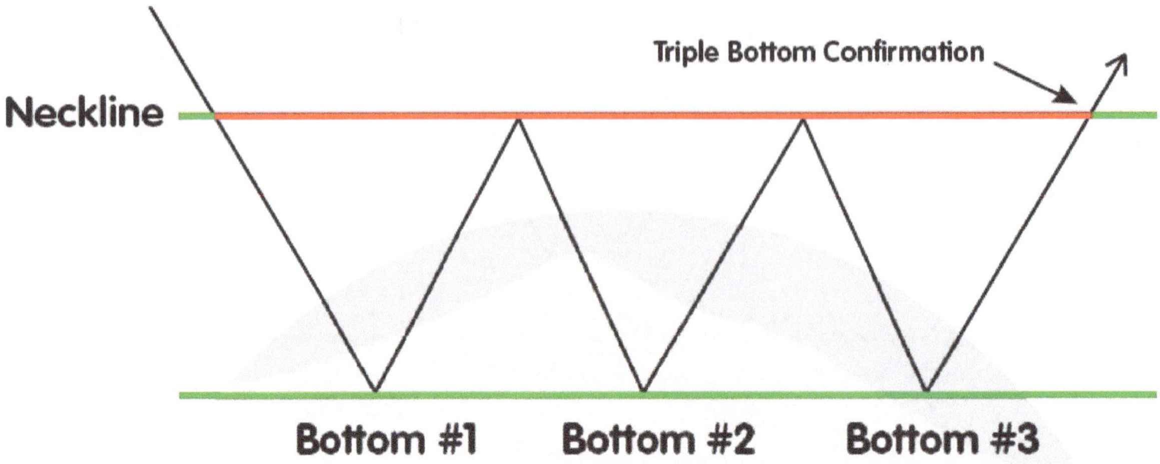

Triple Bottom is a bullish chart pattern used in technical analysis characterized by three identical lows followed by a breakout above a resistance level. -Triple Bottom is a visual pattern that represents buyers (bulls) taking control of the price action from sellers (bears).

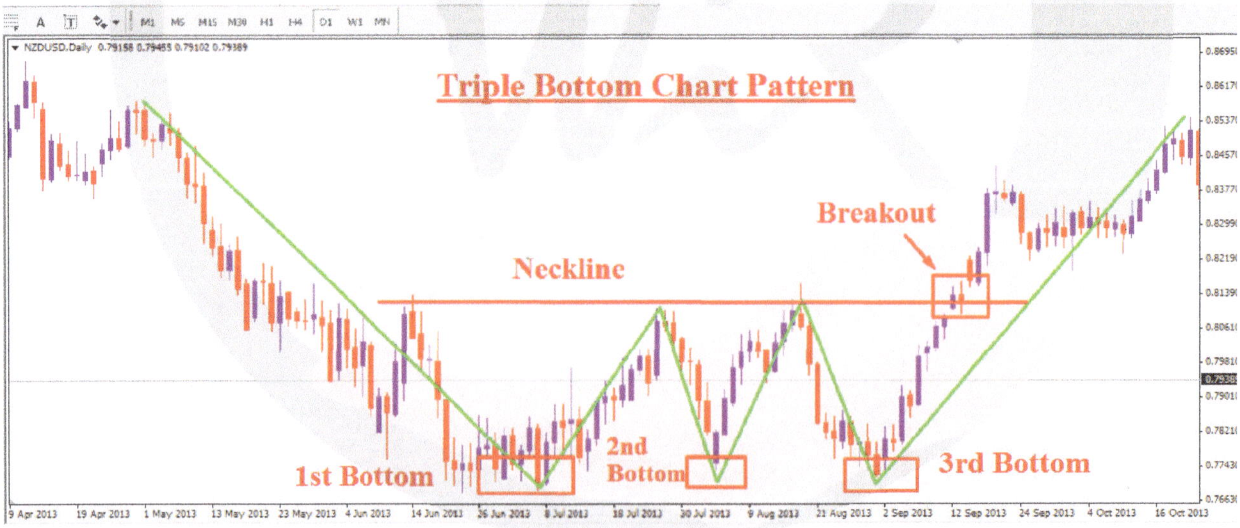

3.5 Bullish Pennant

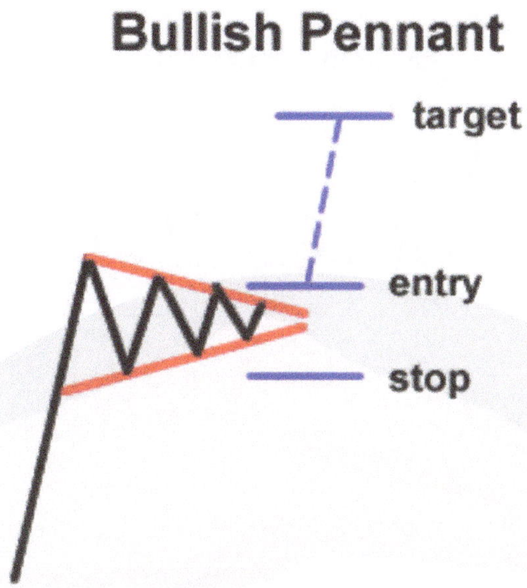

There is a slight difference in the Bullish Pennant Pattern as compared to the Bullish flag pattern. In the pennant pattern, during the consolidation period, both the trend lines do not cross each other at equal distances, but cross each other at a point ahead. After this, when the price breaks the resistance line and moves up, then it is called the Bullish pennant chart pattern.

3.6 Bearish Pennant

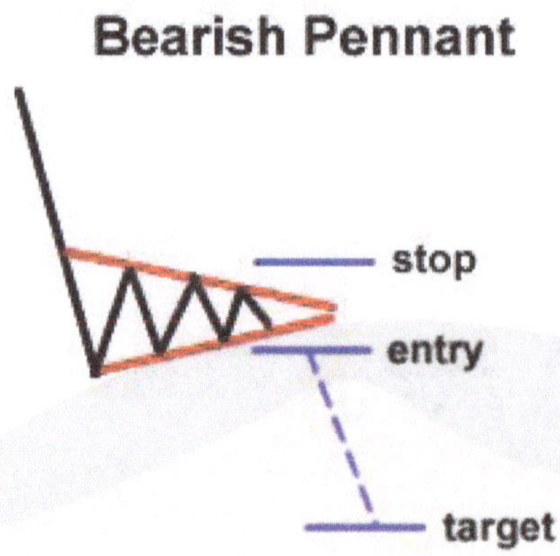

There is a slight difference in the Bearish Pennant pattern as compared to the Bearish flag pattern. In the pennant pattern, during the consolidation period, both the trend lines are not parallel to each other, but they crossover each other at some point ahead. After this, when the price breaks the support line and moves down, then it is called the Bearish Pennant chart pattern and the bearish trend starts again. In this way, the Bearish continuation pennant pattern is formed.

3.7 Bullish Flag

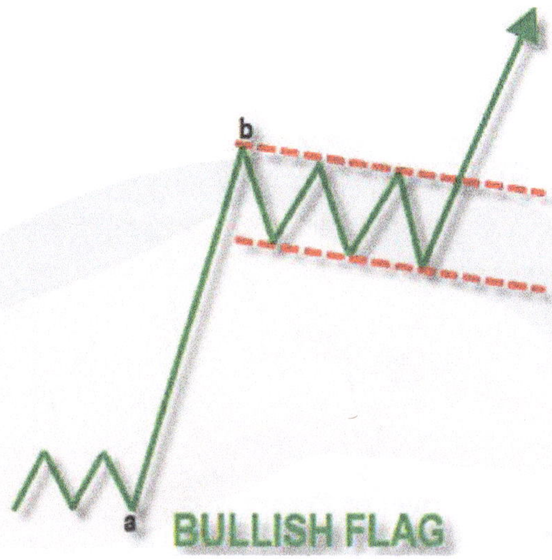

This pattern is formed only when there is a sharp rise in the stock at the beginning. This sharp rise is called the pole of the flag pattern. During a sharp uptrend in the stock, there is higher trading volume than usual. During this time, the price forms a resistance and then the price goes into a consolidation period.

3.8 Bearish Flag

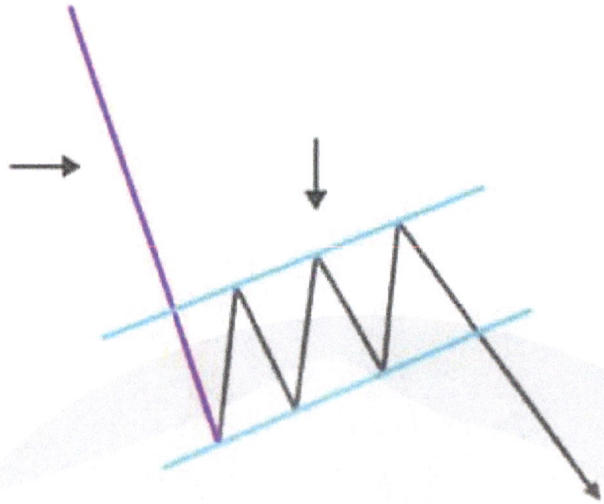

The bearish flag pattern indicates the start of a downtrend in the market after a temporary uptrend ends. That is, the downtrend may continue further. That is, the bears will again try their best to push the price downwards.

3.9 Bullish Rectangle

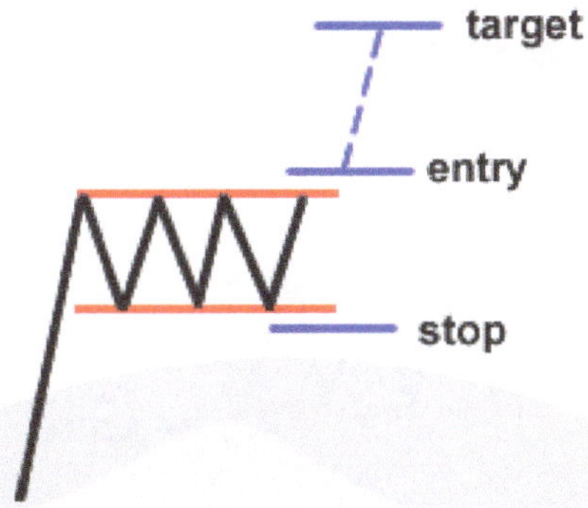

When the price of a stock is going up and falls down after reaching a resistance and after falling a little down it touches the resistance again and does this repeatedly then a box is formed as shown in the image above, this is called Bullish Rectangle Chart Pattern. As soon as the price of the stock breaks the resistance then you can buy the stock and you can keep the stop loss at the center of the box and you can keep your target as much as the difference in the price in the box.

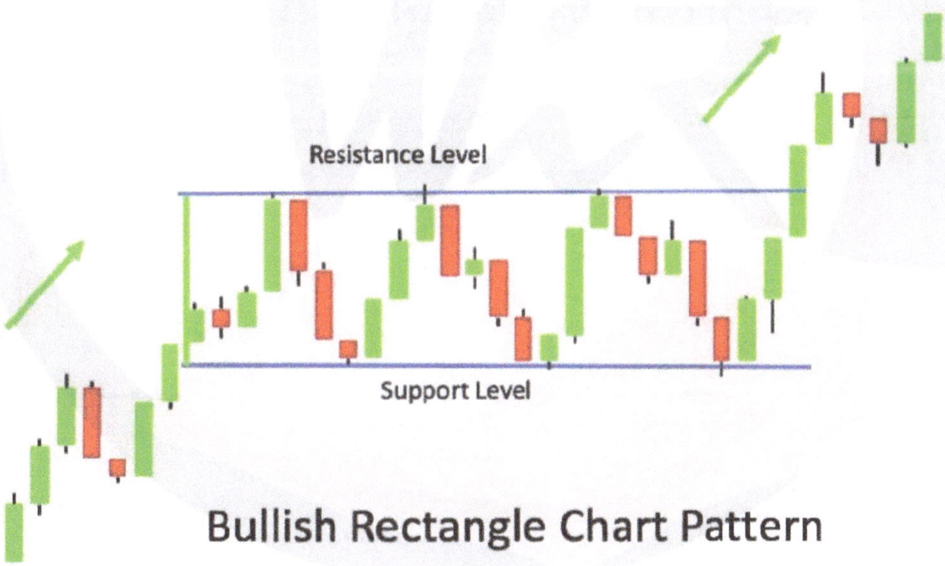

Bullish Rectangle Chart Pattern

3.10 Bearish Rectangle

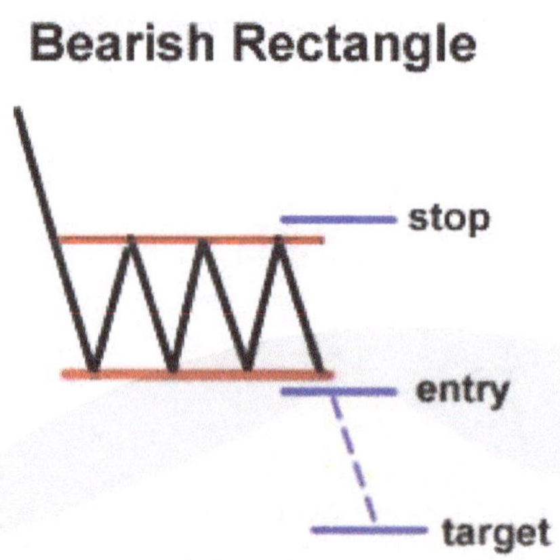

Rectangle chart pattern is formed by drawing two parallel lines. When the market is in down trend, if Rectangle pattern is formed then it indicates Bearish continuation. Meaning this pattern indicates continuation of bearish trend. Hence it is called Bearish Rectangle pattern.

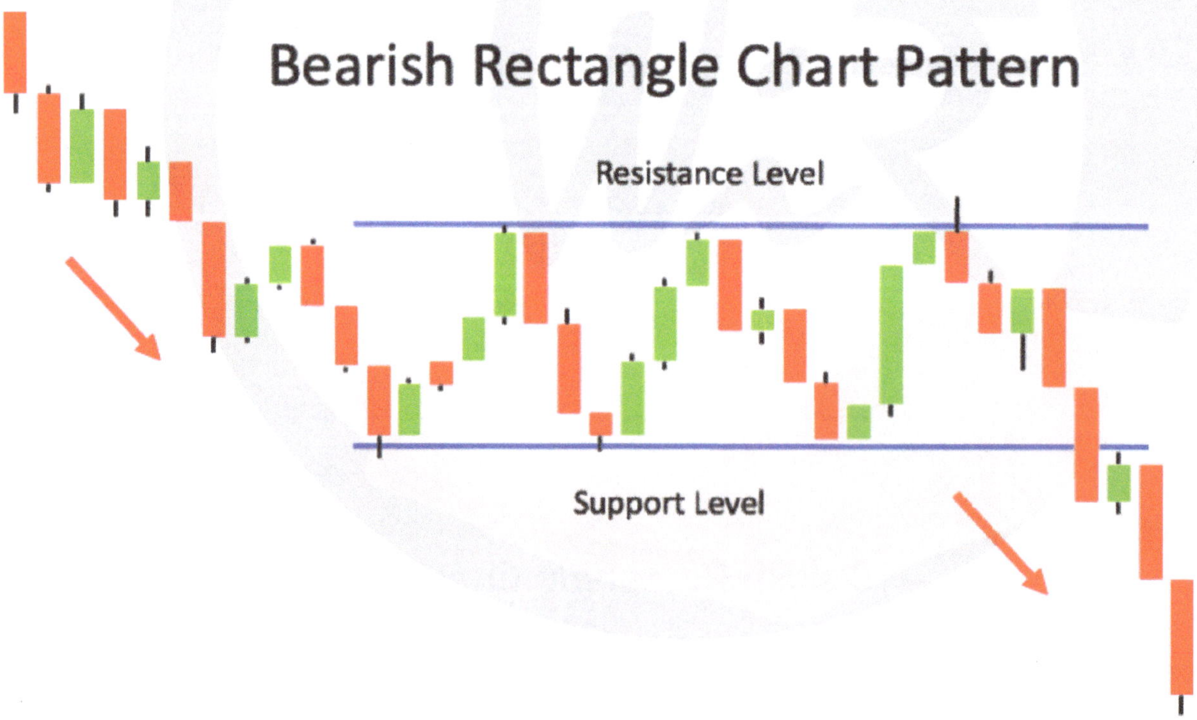

3.11 Rising Wedge

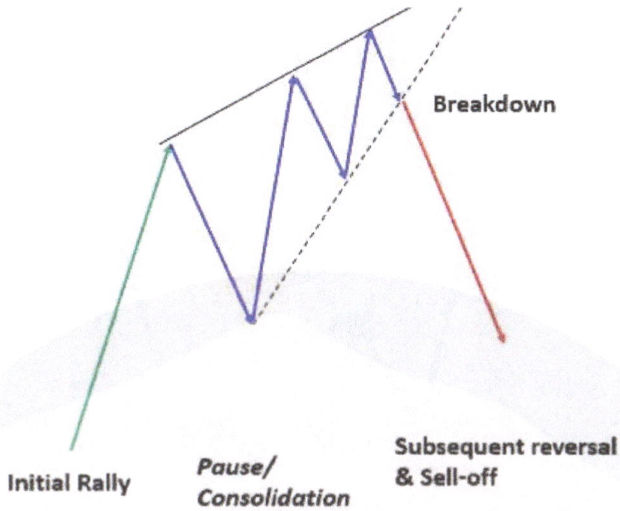

Rising Wedge chart is a bearish chart. It means that after this chart is formed, the period of uptrend in the market or stock is over and the downtrend is about to start. Rising Wedge chart is seen in the uptrend, apart from this if it is seen then it does not work.

Rising Wedge Chart works very well if it is made by taking two or more support and resistance. Rising Wedge Chart gives good results even in intraday.

3.12 Falling Wedge

The falling wedge chart pattern is formed only during a long downtrend. During a long downtrend, the price takes support at the bottom and moves upwards. But this rise forms a resistance nearby and stops there, keeping the downtrend intact.

Many times in such chart pattern, the share price breaks the support trend line and in such a case the share price falls very rapidly. In such a case you can also short the share, if it breaks the resistance trend line, you can buy these shares as soon as it breaks and your stop loss will be the last swing of the support trend line and the target will be 1:2 or you can earn good profit with trailing stop loss.

3.13 Head and Shoulders

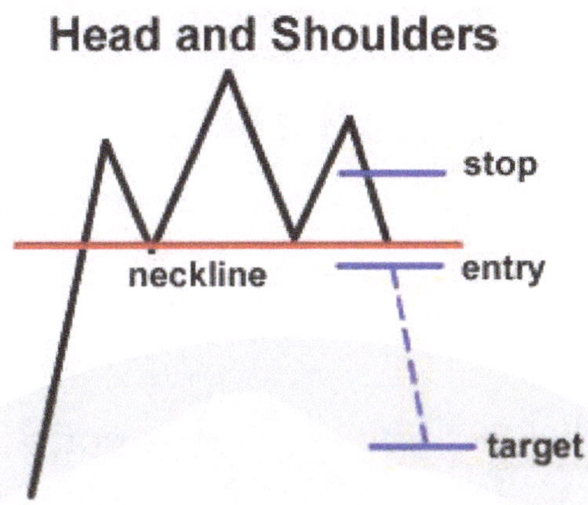

Head and shoulder looks like a man's head and is also called three (3) Buddhas. Head and shoulder is a bearish reversal in a bullish trend. It means that the bullish period is over and recession is about to come.

You will see that head and shoulder chart pattern is being formed in the chart and for the formation of head and shoulder chart it is necessary that the previous trend is up trend.

3.14 Inverted Head and Shoulders

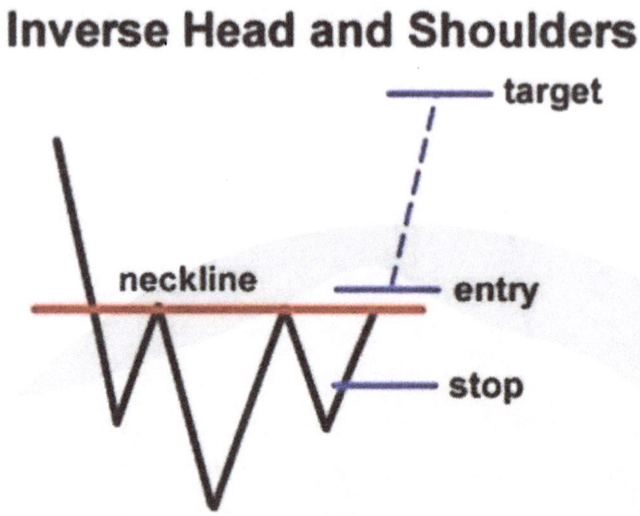

Friends, this pattern looks like an inverted man's head and shoulders in the chart, hence it is named Inverted Head & Shoulder. This pattern is formed after a down trend. This chart pattern indicates Bullish Reversal. Meaning, after the formation of this pattern, there is a sign of a boom in the market. Therefore, it is called Bullish Reversal chart pattern.

3.15 Symmetrical Triangle

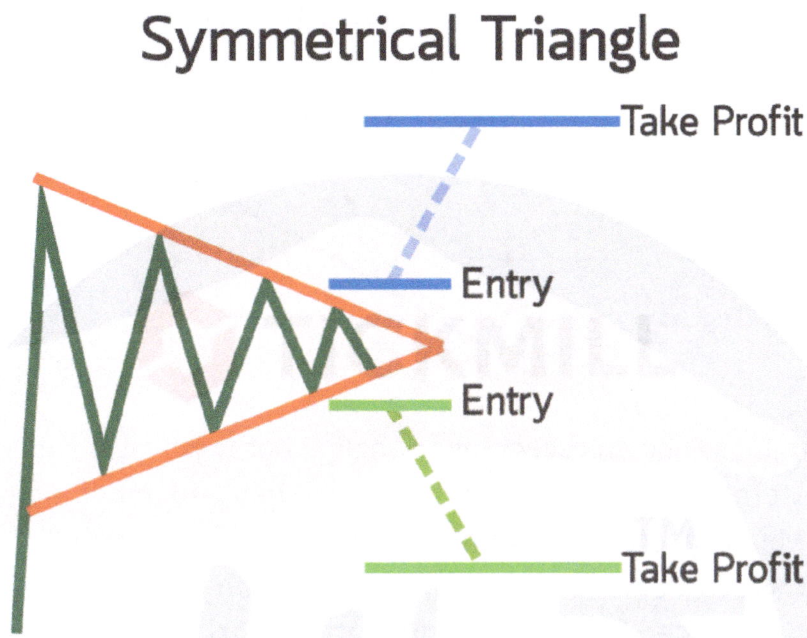

Symmetrical Triangle means symmetrical triangle. This pattern is formed when the price in the market forms a triangle-like pattern. This pattern often works well when it is formed in a sideways market. After the formation of this pattern, the market price starts moving in the direction in which it breaks out or breaks the trend line.

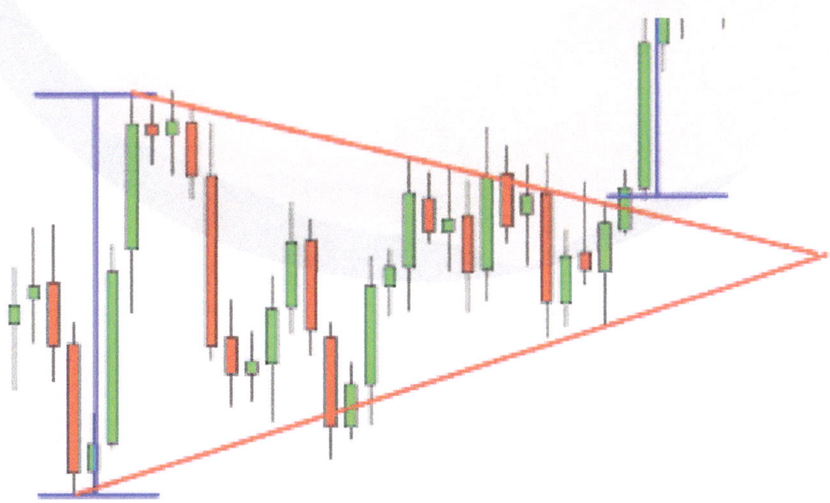

3.16 Ascending Triangle

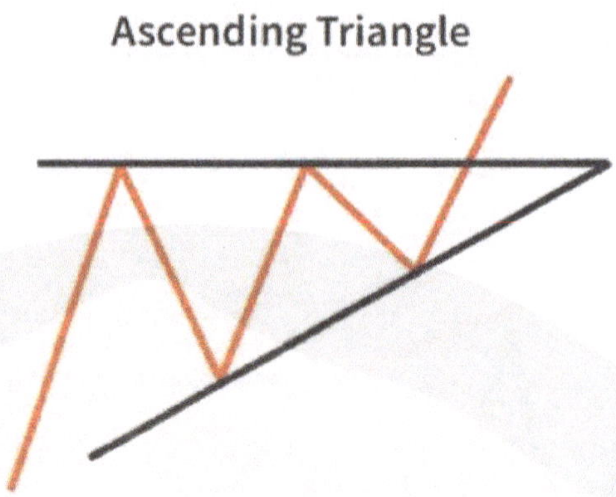

Its chart pattern looks like an ascending triangle. That is why it is called the Ascending triangle pattern. This pattern is formed in the Up trend and it indicates Bullish Continuation. Meaning, after the formation of this pattern, the bullish trend going on in the market will continue further. Such an indication is obtained. That is why it is called the Bullish continuation chart pattern.

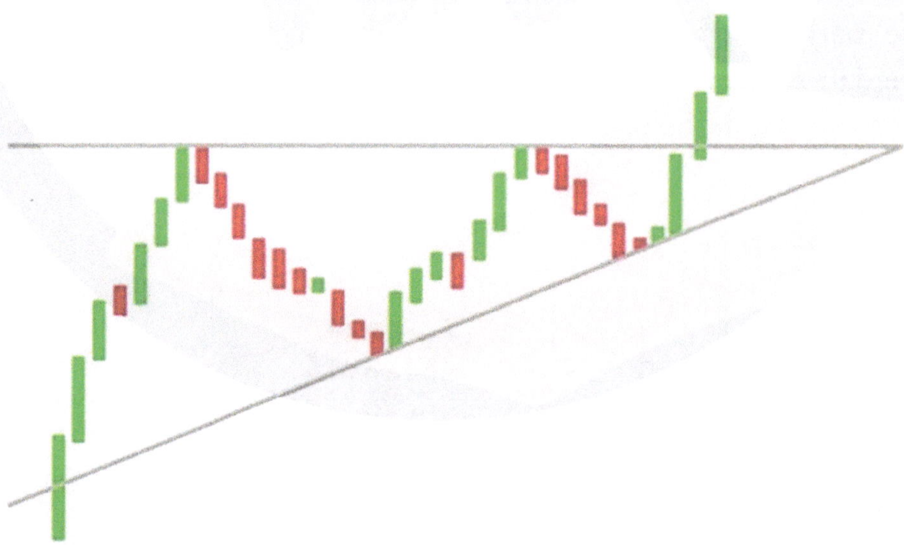

3.17 Descending Triangle

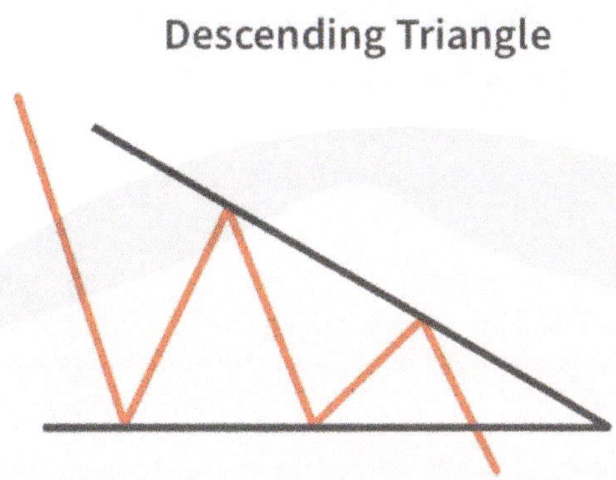

This pattern is formed when stocks make lower highs and the price of all the lower levels is the same. This pattern is usually formed during a downtrend, if this descending pattern is formed during an uptrend then one should be cautious.

3.18 Cup and Handle

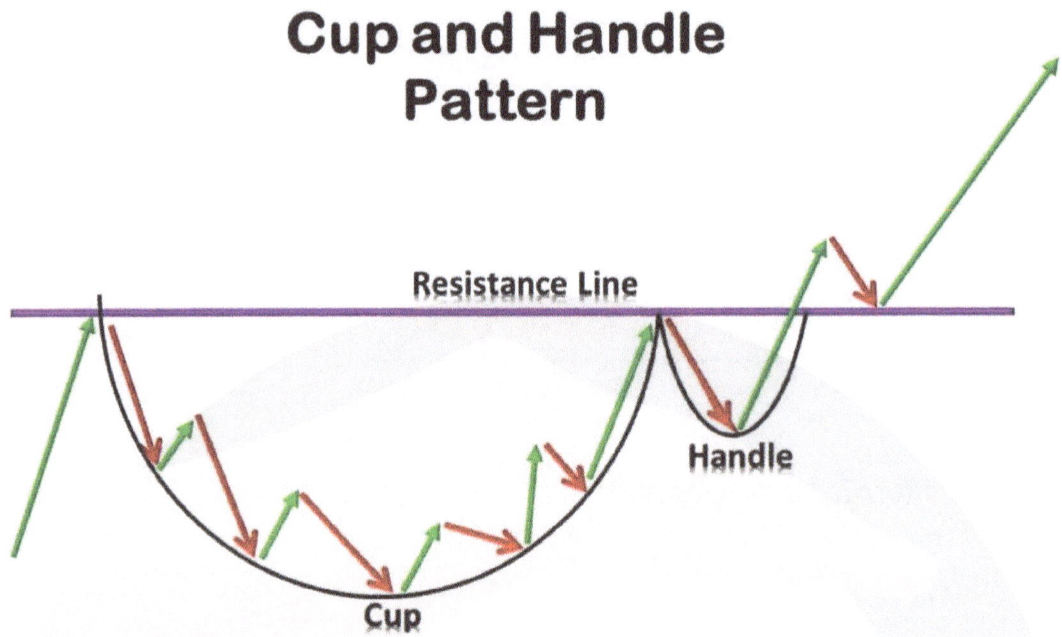

The cup and handle pattern is a bullish continuation pattern that signals a strengthening of the security's price succeeded by a breakout, followed by a further rise in the dividend price. The period of consolidation is the U-shaped cup while the breakout is represented by the handle.

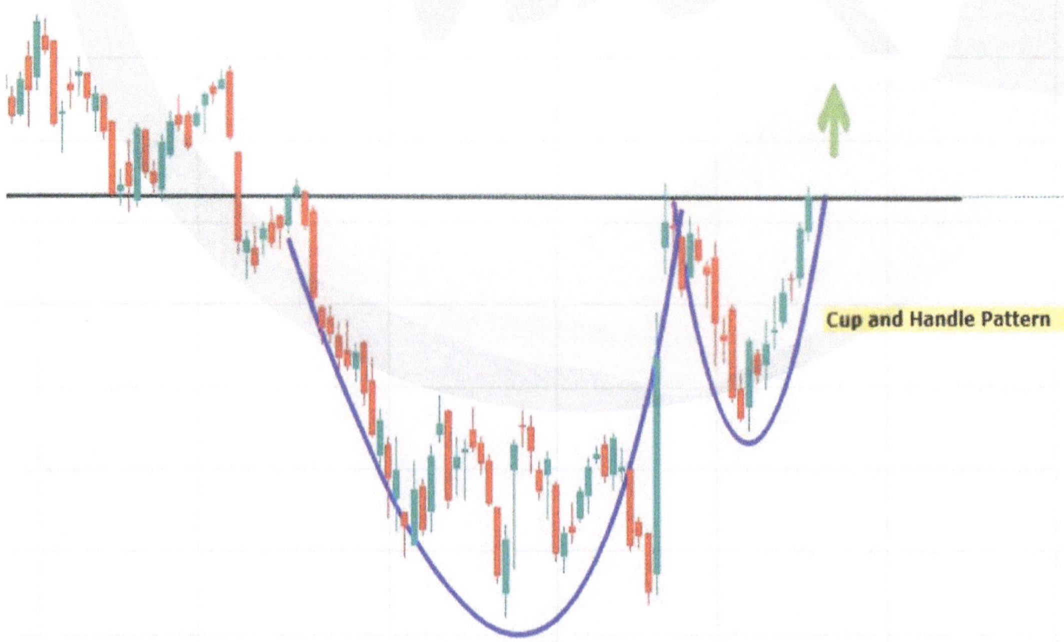

3.19 Rounding Bottom

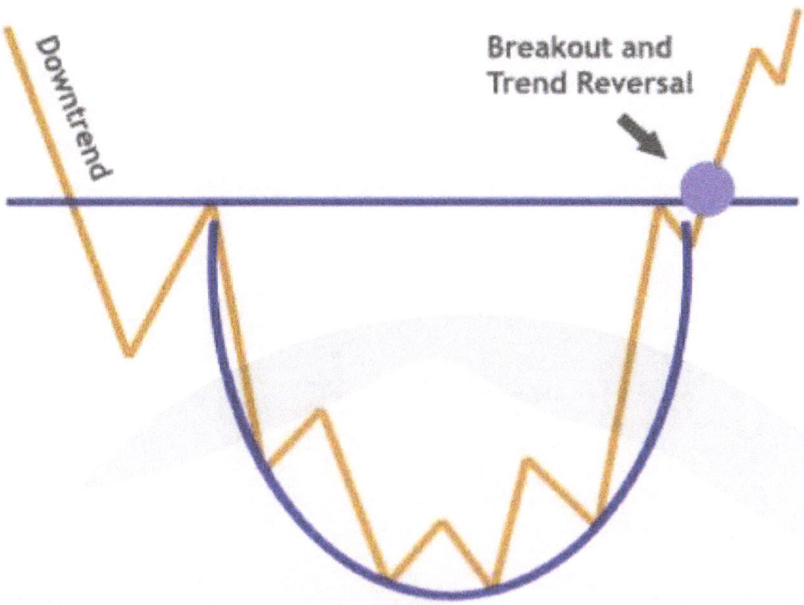

The Rounding Bottom Pattern represents a long-term reversal and is more suitable for weekly charts. Traders may sometimes call it the Saucer Bottom Pattern because it is saucer-shaped.

3.20 Diamond Top

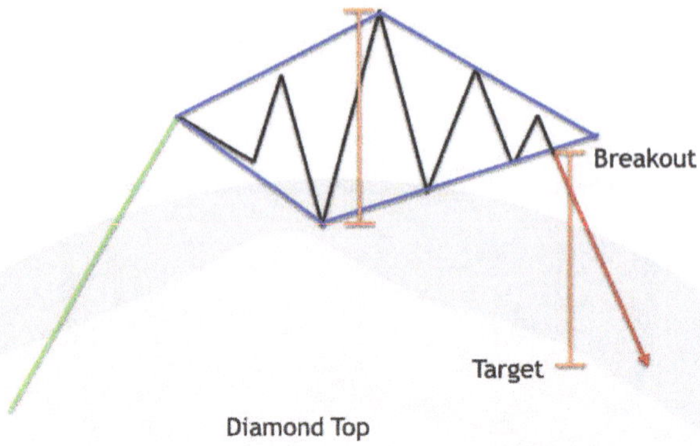

The diamond chart pattern refers to a reversal in the trend in which the stock market forms a pattern that resembles a diamond and signals an upcoming reversal.

3.21 Diamond Bottom

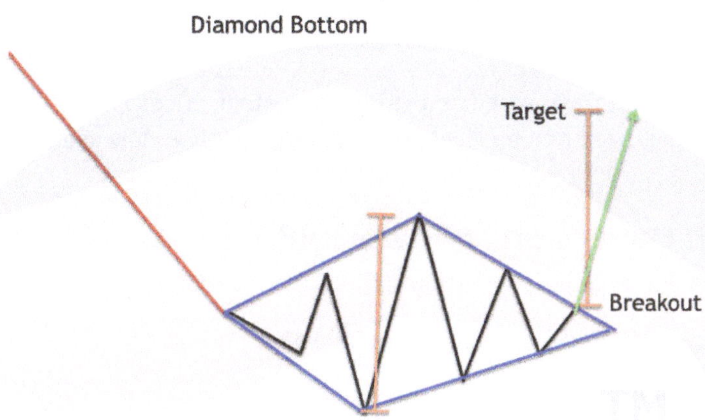

Diamond patterns are advanced chart patterns used to detect trend reversals. Reversal strategies are one of the most profitable trading strategies. They usually occur after long trend phases.

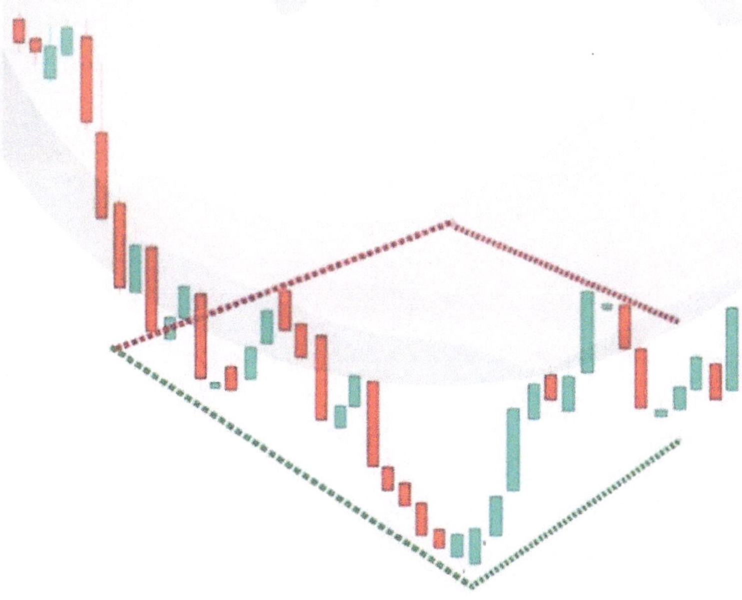

Mean Reversion Trading Strategy

❖ Introduction

Mean reversion is a trading strategy based on the idea that stock prices and returns tend to move back towards their historical average or mean level after deviations. It is widely used in both stocks and commodities.

Why Mean Reversion is Powerful?

- Prices often overreact due to emotions (fear/greed).
- Creates opportunities when markets deviate from fair value.
- Works well in range-bound and sideways markets.
- Highly effective with liquid assets (like indices, blue-chip stocks, and commodities).

Accuracy of Mean Reversion

- In backtests, mean reversion setups typically show **55%–65% win-rate** depending on asset and timeframe.

- With strict risk management, accuracy can be increased.

- Works best when combined with indicators like RSI, Bollinger Bands, VWAP, and Moving Averages.

Indicators Used

1. RSI (Relative Strength Index) – Buy when RSI < 30, Sell when RSI > 70.

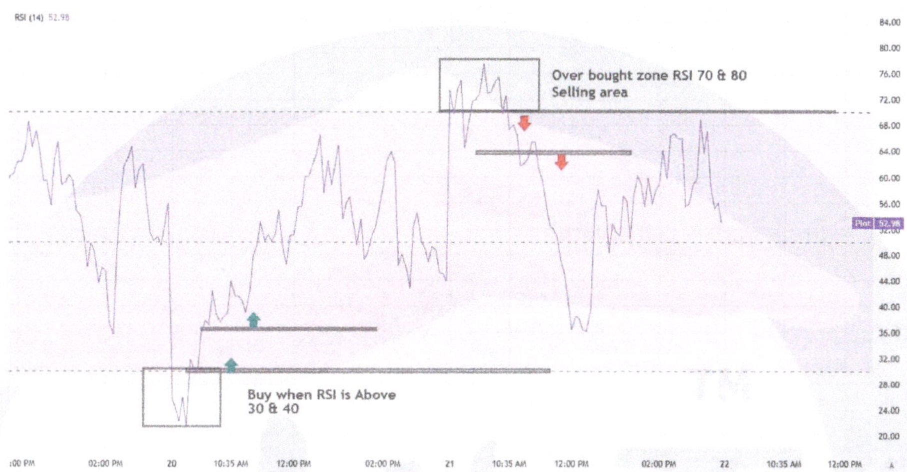

2. Bollinger Bands – Price touches lower band = Buy, upper band = Sell.

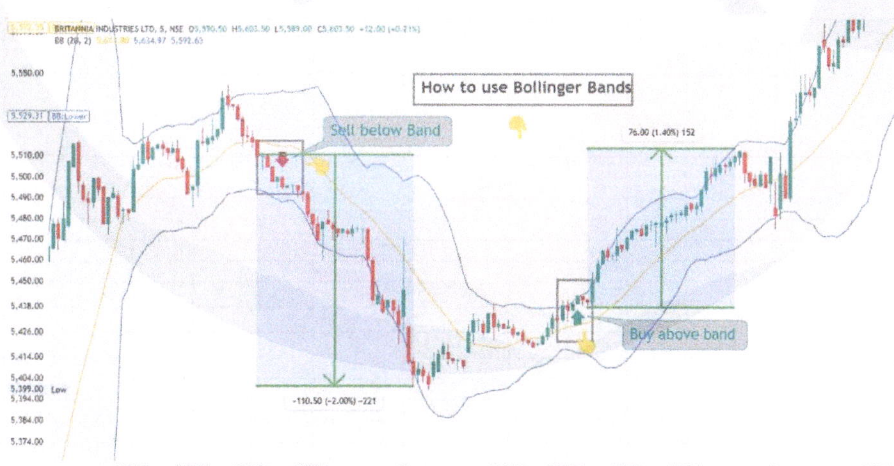

3. VWAP – Entry around deviations from VWAP.

X

4. EMA – Cross Entry & Exit Points.

Example Case Study

For instance, Natural Gas futures falling sharply towards lower support levels and RSI hitting oversold territory can signal a mean reversion bounce back towards EMA or VWAP.

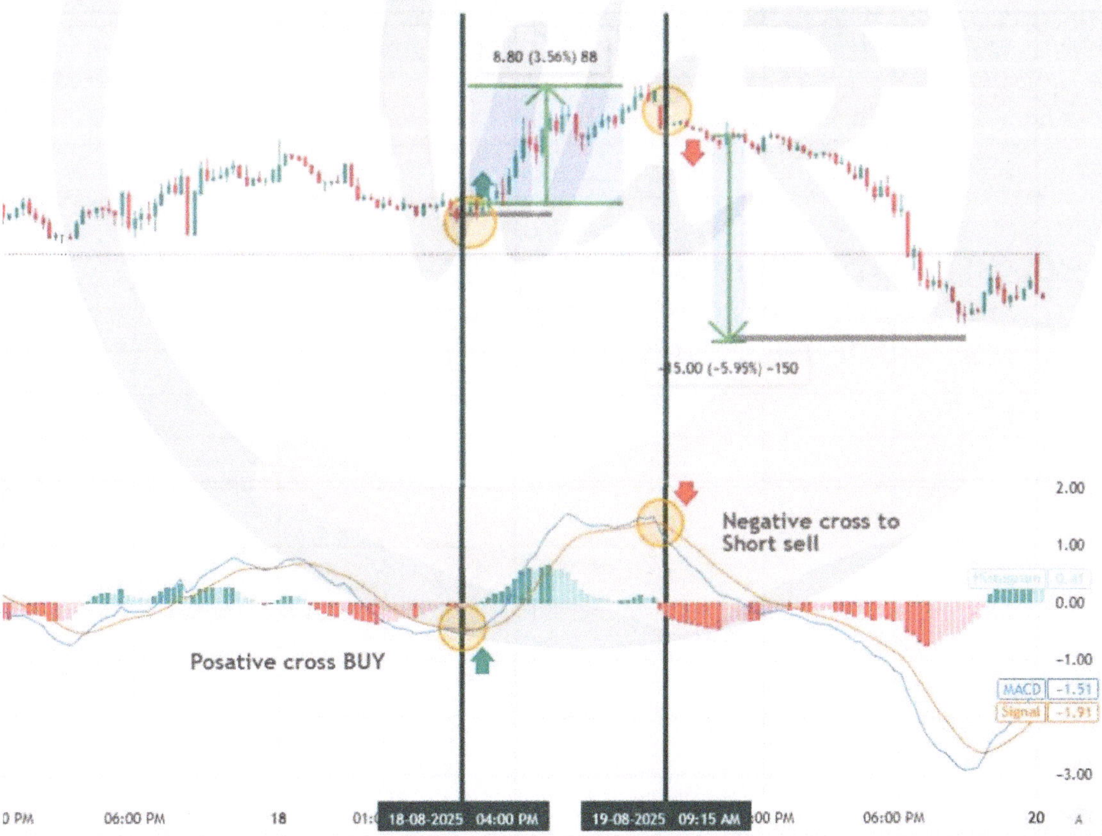

Risk Management

- Always set stop-loss beyond recent swing high/low. - Risk-to-reward ratio should be at least 1:2. Avoid trading during high-impact news releases. - Use position sizing to control losses.

Conclusion

Mean reversion is one of the best setups for traders who prefer high-probability trades with consistent returns. While accuracy ranges around 55–65%, proper discipline, patience, and risk management can make it highly profitable.

Comparison: Leading vs Lagging Indicators

LEADING INDICATORS	LAGGING INDICATORS
• Predict price movement before it happens • Nature: they are oscillators → move faster than price • Strength: great for anticipating reversels or spotting overbought/oversold zones • Weakness: high chance of false signals in sideways/choppy markets	• Confirm price movement after it starts • Nature: They are trend-following indicators → slower than price • Strength: Reduce false signals, give strong confirmation • Weakness: Late entry → you miss the first part of the move

BEST COMBINATION FOR HIGH ACCURACY

RSI → ADX → Leading indicator for entry timing

“The moment you enter the trade”

Before you decide to exit , just think about the reason you took the trade.

Exit the trade if the logic Goes wrong be ruthless about that don’t get attached

Ayush Dixit (Stock market Enthusiast & trader)

“Words of Wisdom”

We all need to understand the concept of trading & investing

Truly based on knowledge we have to buy, keeping our Emotions aside

Pure Dedication Data (fundamental part) Risk management part

Technical part.

Execution part – “follow the rules, If you don’t have entry & exit plan, then don’t trade.”

Hemant pagi (founder Wise investing & placement)

“Control risk, profits will take care of themselves.”

Great traders focus on downside first—upside naturally follows.

“Trading is simple, but not easy.”

Strategies can be taught; mastering your psychology is the real challenge.

THE LOGIC OF TRADING & INVESTING

DATA · DISCIPLINE · DEDICATION · EXECUTION

AYUSH DIXIT
Stock Market Enthusiast & Trader

HEMANT PAGI
Founder, Wise Investing & Placement

WISE INVESTING

Wi₹™